THE TYRANNY OF EXPERTS

THE TYRANNY OF EXPERTS

Blowing the Whistle
on the Cult of Expertise

Morris E. Chafetz, M.D.

MADISON BOOKS
Lanham • New York • London

Published by Madison Books
4720 Boston Way
Lanham, Maryland 20706

3 Henrietta Street
London WC2E 8LU, England

Library of Congress Cataloging-in-Publication Data

Chafetz, Morris E.
The tyranny of experts : blowing the whistle on the cult of
expertise / Morris E. Chafetz.
p. cm.
Includes bibliographical references and index.
1. Professions—Social aspects. 2. Expertise—Social aspects.
I. Title.
HT687.C48 1996 001—dc20 95-50947 CIP

ISBN 1-56833-064-2 (cloth : alk. paper)

Distributed by National Book Network

∞ ™ The paper used in this publication meets the minimum requirements of
American National Standard for Information Sciences—Permanence of
Paper for Printed Library Materials, ANSI Z39.48—1984.
Manufactured in the United States of America.

TO THE CHILDREN OF MY CHILDREN

Drew Edward Chafetz   (Yitzhok ben Zalman)
Maria Caitlin Chafetz   (Simcha bat Zalman)

Benjamin Donovan Chafetz   (Meier ben Odom)
Daniel Addison Chafetz   (Yitzhok ben Odom)

Robin Elizabeth Chafetz   (Rochel bat Dovid)
Alexander Chafetz   (Yitzhok ben Dovid)

Contents

Acknowledgments

A wag once said that stealing the ideas and words of one person is plagiarism; stealing from many people is research. I must be one of the world's greatest researchers! I'm not sure I've ever had an original idea or thought or phrase. What I can do occasionally is put disparate ideas, notions, and phrases into a new perspective. I hope I've done that here. But since so much I read and hear sticks in my head in such strange ways, I cannot give specific attribution and acknowledgment to all of the many writers and other people whose ideas and words I have incorporated in my thinking and writing.

Although the attribution and acknowledgment are anonymous, they are sincere. I publicly acknowledge a lack of pure creativity and acknowledge my deep indebtedness to all of you who have helped me write this book.

I can be specific in my acknowledgment to two people: Lynne Constantine and Marion Chafetz. Lynne has been my collaborator on a number of important projects, and she has collaborated with me in fashioning this book. Marion is my wife, and although many authors acknowl-

ix

edge the patience and understanding of their spouses, my wife's position for the past twenty years has been that and more. Marion provided a crucial ingredient to this book: reality. My colleagues and I can become so enthusiastic and self-absorbed in a project that reality can sometimes elude us. Marion brings us back to earth from our enthusiastic flights into space, and the value to this book of her contribution is immeasurable.

But when all is said and done, the faults are mine and the criticisms should be directed only to me.

Morris E. Chafetz, M.D.
(Moishe ben Yitzhok)

Preface

On an airplane flight just after the birth of my first grandchild in 1983, I struck up a conversation with the stranger
sitting beside me and soon found myself rhapsodizing
about the new baby. The man, a father himself, listened
quietly until I ran out of steam, then said, "I hope you're
taking steps to protect him."

"Protect him from what?" I asked.

The stranger then told me a harrowing story. A four-
year-old girl shopping with her mother at Bloomingdales
vanished while her mother was distracted for a few seconds.
Discovering her daughter's absence, the mother rushed to
a security guard, who alerted the store security force. Exits
were sealed. Every adult leaving with a young girl was
stopped and questioned. The mother began to despair,
until a cry of terror drew her attention to a small boy being
led firmly out of the building by a tall couple. In a matter
of minutes, the couple had cut the missing girl's hair,
changed her clothes, and disguised her as a boy.

"Believe me, this goes on all the time," my seat partner
assured me, concluding his story with a series of alarming
statistics. "You've got to take precautions."

I grabbed his sleeve. "What can I do?"

He suggested, among other high-tech remedies, a tiny radio transmitter that could be embedded in a child's tooth. I came home convinced that I would buy one, or something like it. No grandchild of mine would disappear without a trace, not if I had anything to say about it.

A few days later, while my emotions were still in an uproar, I turned on a television program about child kidnapping and heard quite a different story. An FBI agent, one of the bureau's leading experts on child abduction, stated that in the entire United States, only sixty-four children had been kidnapped by strangers in the previous year. The vast majority of child abductions, he explained, are related to child-custody disputes and are carried out by one of the child's parents.

I do not think the solicitous stranger was deliberately misleading me. I think he was himself misled. Someone had hooked him by engaging one of his most primitive emotions: the desire to protect his family. He, in turn, had hooked me the same way.

I should have known better than to take his version of the facts without questioning. For most of my professional life, I have been involved in the study of an emotionally charged subject: people's relations with alcohol beverages. As a public servant and as a private citizen, I have seen what emotional investment in a subject can do to anyone's objectivity. I have seen alcohol researchers literally shout down each other with conflicting interpretations of the same data. I have seen the preliminary results of small, uncontrolled research studies blazoned across the front pages of newspapers as incontrovertible fact. I have seen impressive-looking but essentially meaningless statistical charts and graphs accompanying major articles in prestigious scientific journals.

When it comes to subjugating objectivity to the service of emotion, I've seen a lot of it done. From time to time, I've done it myself; but I didn't recognize the seduction when it was done to me.

My experience at thirty-five thousand feet continues to haunt me. If I, a physician, a psychiatrist, once head of a powerful government agency, with long-time ties to the academic and government worlds of science and statistics, can be so misled, what about people who have not had such rigorous training? How do they make sense of the cacophony of voices giving conflicting advice about every subject imaginable? Health. Nutrition. Child rearing. Alcohol. Drugs. Safe food. Pollution. Who has the answers?

I believe this question is the most important one of our day. Many people believe *someone* does, in fact, have answers that they do not possess. Because they want to believe in that magical "someone," they are defenseless against those who claim to have special knowledge. They are fair game for anyone who offers them comforting certainties, unambiguous rules of conduct, and ways to identify themselves within the complex, fast-moving society we live in. Awash in prescriptions and proscriptions but lacking a means of judging the validity of what they hear, they soon find themselves ruled by a tyranny of experts.

By "expert," I'm not referring to the multitudes of people who possess specialized knowledge and use it to keep the gears of our society working: plumbers, engineers, court reporters, airline pilots, game wardens, truckers, botanists, dieticians, computer programmers. All these people possess valuable technical expertise in their own fields and use it to our collective benefit.

The people I call tyrants are people who overstep the limits of their technical expertise and use their specialized knowledge to dictate how others should live. In our world of instant communication, we know who these experts are. Many are scientists, public interest advocates, researchers, lawyers, physicians, psychologists, social workers, government bureaucrats, and others who, through our mass media, parlay their credentials into power bases. From these power bases, they tell us what to eat, drink, and enjoy, how to relate to one another, and how to live.

The pronouncements of experts fill the moral and ethical vacuum left by the demise of the extended family and the waning of religious and political leadership. In many areas where basic values and personal views of the world once helped people make choices, they now turn to experts for what they believe is definitive information. In a world reeling from the dizzying pace of growth and change, being told what to eat, how much sleep to get, and how to rear children gives people a semblance of certainty that is difficult to come by anywhere else.

Because the experts fill a genuine need for order in the chaotic whirl of high-tech, high-speed living, some of us remain stunningly blind to their pervasive, invasive encroachment on the prerogatives of our private lives, as well as to the possibility that something besides pure benevolence motivates their actions. Our innate self-protectiveness is disarmed but not broken. That characteristic American prickliness, for example, comes to the fore when we learn that the video store's computer keeps a record of all the videos we rent.

The potential misuse of such information violates our privacy and conjures up images of Big Brother and the "thought police" of George Orwell's novel *Nineteen Eighty-Four*. To me, a far more chilling prospect is the surrender of our right to choose in return for promises of happiness and harmony, as in the fictional society described by Aldous Huxley in *Brave New World*. We are learning that the most powerful tyrant of all is one who possesses the consent of the tyrannized.

I distrust expertise not just because an alarmist on an airplane duped me, but because I know where the experts are coming from. I've been there. I know what it feels like to seek an identity in the comforting initials you can place after your signature. I sought my identity by going to medical school. Then, in the days of quotas, admission was an impossible dream for a Jewish kid of modest ability. The initials "M.D." after my name have been a continuous, comforting identifier for me for almost fifty years.

Even my entry into the field of alcoholism treatment was in large measure a quest for status and identity. Through a fortuitous acquaintance with the brilliant mathematician Norbert Wiener, known as the "father of cybernetics," I got a position at Harvard Medical School and Massachusetts General Hospital. To remain there during a time of reorganization, I took on a job no other psychiatrist would have touched: running a state-funded alcoholism treatment clinic at the hospital.

My taking the job was an act of supreme self-serving smugness. In truth, I was not interested in the plight of alcoholics. I had the worst kinds of preconceived notions about them. They were bums, I thought, who had chosen their miserable lot in life. But opportunist that I was, I took the job.

Fortunately for me and for those whom I treated, I soon found that I could not maintain my blind biases when I was face-to-face with these troubled human beings. In fact, I soon discovered that these so-called dregs of humanity were generous, genuine people who brought me an extraordinary opportunity for personal growth and learning. My work in the field of alcoholism has taught me more about how people relate to one another in society than I learned in all my previous training.

When the nation decided in the 1970s to rethink its collective biases about alcoholism and alcoholic people, I was invited to become the first director of the National Institute on Alcohol Abuse and Alcoholism in the Health, Education, and Welfare Department. The experience as head of a powerful government agency taught me another valuable lesson: I found that I was not immune to the seductiveness of power. I learned how hungry I was for it; how tenaciously I would fight for it; how desperate I was to maintain it; and how glibly I could justify stepping on others to get it. I also learned the sad lesson of its ephemeral nature. When I left government, I went quickly from "Who's Who" to "Who's He."

My experiences have taught me to understand experts from the inside out. I lived in their skin. I know what motivates them. I know their strategies and tactics. That's why I fear them and their growing influence over American life and thought.

I've written this book because I believe we are in danger of surrendering our intellectual and emotional liberty to those who would warn, advise, and guide us: people who manipulate us with their specialized knowledge and increasingly determine the political, moral, and social climate of our country. I fear the brave new world their tactics threaten to bring upon us. I want us to regain our right to think for ourselves by withdrawing our consent to their ascendancy.

The irony of our surrender to the experts is that they don't even deliver the peace of mind they promise. Ask yourself a simple question: do you truly feel safer, saner, and more secure because of everything you've been told by the health experts, the environmental experts, the legal experts, the child development experts, the crime experts, the alcohol experts? Or are you becoming more fearful? More anxious about your health? Less secure about your abilities as a spouse, a child, a parent? Less confident about the future?

To help you gain perspective on what you hear and read, I intend to share with you what I know about these experts. I realize that this book could be seen as a hypocritical exercise—whistle-blowing on experts by an expert. Unlike those experts who tyrannize, my goal here is to inform the reader, not to conform the reader.

In the subsequent chapters, you'll meet the fearmongers and the conformity seekers, the manipulators and the protectionists, the crusaders and the lambs, the deluders and the self-deluders. You'll read about abuse in the areas of medicine, technology, advocacy, ecology, and of course in my own field, alcohol. A thorough airing of the manipulations of experts in any area, especially those in which I believe the experts have gained their greatest victory at our expense, is beneficial.

I hope this book will reveal a new angle on experts and their expertise—one that will give you a sense of control over your world and a renewed confidence in yourself. I want to make it clear, however, that many experts are motivated by their concern for humanity. I believe that we as a society have given them power over our lives and our thoughts, because we want what they profess to give us: definitive answers for the troubling questions of life.

Daniel Defoe wrote, "All men would be tyrants if they could." This book attempts to expose the prestidigitation of experts whose purpose is to hold sway over our lives, confounding our ability to discover insights for ourselves.

Chapter 1

Ascendancy through Fear

A hospital advertisement shows a woman giving herself a breast exam. The caption says, "This woman just missed the cancer that will kill her."

This advertisement for a mammography unit in a California hospital won its creators a prestigious advertising award, and I can understand why. It is diabolically unforgettable. In one stark image, the ad instills mortal terror in any woman who worries about breast cancer, and instills doubt in many women who formerly did not. Simultaneously, it abolishes all hope of having any personal control. Its implied message says, "You are in imminent danger. If you try to help yourself, you will guarantee your own demise. Depend on us to protect you."

Welcome to the world of the medical experts. Physicians, health professionals, and biomedical researchers greatly influence our health decisions because we believe they hold in their hands our most precious possession—our lives.

This ad is a flagrant example of how the medical establishment preys on our health concerns. It hopes to ensure its dominance over the realm of health care by invoking the primordial fear of death and promising security and comfort. When such powerful emotions are artfully manipu-

1

lated, people readily succumb to a dependent role. Caught on an endless treadmill of new health worries, people are linked umbilically to the self-interest of the medical profession.

End to Self-Care

Make no mistake, this ad and the increasing number of others like it are not just a continuation of the omnipresent health warnings of the 1970s and 1980s that fostered what Michael Schrage of the *Los Angeles Times* calls the state of "bionarcissism": an urgent preoccupation with one's own well-being.

Bionarcissists jog, own blood pressure machines, and ride stationary bikes. They shun red meat and worry about the minute doses of radiation they receive from dental X rays. They expect their physicians to spend time educating them about lifestyle issues, and they are not afraid to shop around for a physician who meets their standards.

Despite the pejorative sound of the term, bionarcissism isn't all bad. People believe that they can maintain or improve their own health with simple, commonsense changes in lifestyle such as no smoking, more exercise, better diet, and lower weight. These practices did help reduce the death rate from cardiovascular disease by over 25 percent between 1950 and 1985.

Both the lowered incidence of deaths from cardiac disease and the willingness of people to make simple changes in lifestyle prompted the medical profession to incorporate the self-care movement. The medical experts don't mind if people avoid red meat, but they definitely do not like the idea of self-care. They want the bionarcissists to be dependent on the health-care system.

One example of how practicing physicians assimilate the self-care movement is seen in the new trend toward physician-operated health-promotion services. Albeit long overdue, health promotion was grudgingly accepted by doctors who, by and large, cared only about treating existing disease, not about taking measures to prevent disease. Today, many physicians now operate nutrition-counseling services, stop-smoking clinics, and weight-control services as part of their practices. These programs are prescribed for patients who want these special services. Frequent office visits are required.

Part of the reason for discouraging an independent course of self-care is simple economics. Physicians are businesspeople interested in the bottom line. Despite society's repeated attempts to make health-care providers more businesslike and more cost conscious, health-care costs continue to rise. At the present time, health-care costs are over 14 percent of the gross domestic product (GDP). This percentage is the highest in the world. Although the United States is the world's richest nation, it spends far more of its income on health care than any other country. According to the United Nation's 1994 Human Development Report, people in other countries live longer and get more care.

Pushing and pulling, many interests are at work. Political pressure to control health-care costs continues to mount. Health-care providers, however, fight cost cuts, claiming that high-tech medical care is expensive but indispensable. Consumers want insurance coverage for more procedures, including care for the less fortunate. The jobs, perquisites, social prestige, and personal power of thousands of scientists, physicians, health-care executives, and allied health professionals depend on maintaining the popular belief that only the medical care system can heal sickness and bestow health.

Chapter One

Lure of Dependency

The health-care marketing strategy of the 1990s, as illustrated by the mammography advertisement, is based on society's deep-seated belief in the certitude of experts, especially where the physical and mental health of the body is concerned. I observed this fact recently when my forty-two-year-old son had a midwinter attack of poison ivy. On my advice he went to see his family doctor, but the itching, swelling, and burning from the rash continued in spite of treatment.

He asked me for more medical advice; when I didn't have any for him, he became unusually angry with me. Rationally, my son knew that poison ivy runs its course or responds to treatment; but in his heart, he wanted his father to make it all better for him. He was looking to the first expert who had comforted him and soothed his fears with a definitive answer, even if it was a made-up answer.

As children, most of us learn to depend on our parents for answers and comfort. Many parents take care of every need; they calm their children's fears; they kiss away the pain of a scraped knee; and they always, always seem to have answers to the question, "why?" That indoctrinated belief in answers and assurance from those first experts follows many people into adulthood. Some of us depend on experts, in this case the medical profession, to become like parents, to soothe our fears and rid us of our adult nagging uncertainties.

Death, Fear, and the Promised Land

Most of us become aware of death at an early age, when a relative or a pet dies. At first, the concept of death may not be fully understood; but in time, the realization that the person or pet no longer exists in the physical world becomes clear. At that point we begin to make a personal connection between death and ourselves. Once we make this connection, we devote much of our mental energy to strategies for avoiding death. These strategies manifest themselves in a variety of ways. Religion is a favored comforter. It tempers the fear of oblivion by promising the hope of an afterlife.

Unquestioning faith in doctors and the power of medicine has also been a favored balm for the fear of death. With the medical profession's seemingly intimate connection to the mysteries of life and death, doctors have long enjoyed a godlike aura.

From the earliest shaman to today's neurologist, doctors and their forebears have distracted us from the fear of death with prognostication and medication. Their job is often made easier when pain and illness produce regressive (child-like) behavior. When we regress we are more vulnerable to the magic of formulas and symbols. What makes us easy prey to regressive behavior is what Ernest Becker contends in his book *Fear of Death*—that our greatest fear is the certainty of our own death.

When the self-help, self-care movement began in the 1950s, nonmedical people such as Adele Davis (*Let's Eat Right to Keep Fit*) and Robert Rodale (*Prevention* magazine) took away from the medical profession some of its mystique. Norman Cousins, former editor of the *New Republic*, for example, when struck with an illness his doctors thought was fatal, swore that laughing at old comedies did more to cure his life-threatening illness than his physicians did. However, in spite of the acceptance of the self-help movement, the waning years of the twentieth century show a return to an investiture in the physician's omnipotence.

5

The belief by many people in the infallibility of the doctor gives them hope that they may yet be able to cheat death. As a doctor, I can say with assurance that the aura of omnipotence has always been cultivated by the medical profession. That's why the words "medical miracle" heralded the following innovations: genetic engineering, MRI machines, infertility treatments, organ transplants, neonatal intensive care units, and other manifestations of high-tech medicine.

The placebo effect is another manifestation of the belief in medical omnipotence. The placebo effect is based on faith, hope, and a lot of charity. People get better because they believe they will. However, the opposite effect is equally powerful: people get sick because they believe they will.

Early in my career I treated and studied people with Parkinson's disease. I was interested in learning how emotions affect the progress of the disease. One day a patient excitedly told me how much better she was doing with the new medicine I had prescribed. I was startled by this news, because I had not prescribed any new medication. I called the hospital pharmacist to see what was going on. The pharmacist told me that the pharmaceutical company had changed the shape and color of the medicine.

Nothing was different. It was the same medication at the same dosage that the patient had been taking for years. Yet the patient believed she was taking a new medicine, and this led to her reported improvement—the placebo effect.

Variations of this fascinating story are a common occurrence in and out of medicine. Studies have shown that even with placebos—fake pills—over 33 percent of a group being treated may show improvement.

The *Wall Street Journal*, in an extensive front-page article, pointed out how a family-owned company had found a lucrative niche producing health-food pills. By downing bodybuilding capsules, multiple dietary supplements, all-purpose vitamin mixtures, and antiaging compounds, the gullible public is making the company rich. Not only is the company making money, but it also does not have to face the regulatory scrutiny of the Food and Drug Administration. Moreover, there are no credible studies that prove either the efficacy or the danger of these products, but the power of suggestion and expectation (the placebo effect) is used to good business advantage. Manipulating a gullible public has always been the province of snake-oil sales-people.

Expectation is the most powerful element of the placebo effect. Each new transfer of knowledge between human beings—from the first scratchings of cave-dwellers to computer e-mail—increases our belief that somehow the outcome of our lives will be different. Yes, our lives will be different, but our outcome will not. All that live must die.

In 1952, shortly after I came to Massachusetts General Hospital, I found myself drawn to areas of study in which psychiatry overlaps neurology. I had the opportunity to work with Robert Schwab, a pioneer in the "miracle" technology for understanding the brain, the electroencephalogram (EEG).

Soon after I had begun to learn the new technology, the entire staff of the EEG lab left to attend a conference, leaving me on-call to interpret EEGs during their absence. I asked Schwab, "Isn't it dangerous to leave someone as inexperienced as I to be the expert interpreter of an EEG? What if a surgeon opens someone's head on the basis of my interpretation?" Schwab simply smiled. "Morris, if anyone is going to do brain surgery on the basis of an EEG finding alone, they were going to do it regardless of what you said the EEG shows."

I was comforted by his answer then, but it makes me highly uncomfortable now. Did Schwab mean that once a physician has reached a conclusion, the physician is neither deterred nor advanced by any other information? Did he mean that these physicians by using this "miracle technology" were going though the rituals of looking for objective information (if there is such a thing) but allowed their belief systems to rule no matter what the facts?

I am not saying that working from instinct is necessarily always bad. Brilliant diagnosticians learn more from listening to a patient than other physicians learn from a complete battery of tests. A physician treating my wife for rheumatoid arthritis nearly killed her by following a cookbook approach to her care, though he ran every test and kept up with the latest research on miracle drugs. The physician who restored her to her current state of health and function did just one thing differently: he listened to her and took seriously everything she told him about her reactions to the treatments he prescribed.

A highly respected judge in Virginia once told the Virginia Bar Association, "A good judge decides a case on the basis of a gut feeling, then finds the legal precedents to support his or her instincts." I have no quarrel with that approach. What I do have a quarrel with is the mystification and mumbo jumbo, the veneer of objectivity with which most experts, physicians among them, cloak their subjectivity. I have no problem with people acting on their belief systems, unless those belief systems are presented as objective fact to manipulate me, you, or anyone else.

When we are sick, most of us don't care to inquire how our physician reaches the conclusion that we have X disease and not Y disease. We simply want comfort and certainty. We want the doctor to tell us we will not die. We want to believe that the miracle of technology and the wisdom of the doctor are great enough to forecast the future and to control all the variables that can affect our health and well-being. But that can't be. No one is that omnipotent. Tragic examples abound of the unabashed trust people put in doctors' omnipotence.

The psychological variable, for instance, and its impact on the immune system and other disease-prevention mechanisms cannot be measured. My brother-in-law Sidney, for example, practiced general medicine in New York City. In the late thirties he was part of a small group of physicians who started the Health Improvement Program (HIP), a forerunner of the health maintenance organizations of today. During the depression, HIP provided inexpensive medical care to people who did not have other access to care.

Sidney enjoyed his association with the pioneer organization. In a way, HIP helped to fulfill the goals of many doctors who entered medicine when it was a noble profession. Well into the first third of the twentieth century, medicine was less about expertise and more about compassion; and physicians had little more in their black bags than caring and concern. In the case of my brother-in-law, his emotional ties to HIP allowed him to practice medicine as a truly dedicated doctor.

He was a walker before walking became fashionable, and he took long, fast-paced walks twice a day. He ate the right foods. He was thin. Yet six weeks after he was forced out of HIP, he suffered a heart attack. He died a few months later. Although I can't prove cause and effect, I believe that the loss of his association with HIP mortally wounded his sense of self-worth and caused his death. This loss was a variable that no doctor, test, or piece of equipment could measure or foresee.

The formulas we associate with good health do not

always contain the essential ingredients. Just as we cannot foresee the future, doctors cannot measure or control hidden variables when they make their pronouncements. But recent technological advances have so intensified our fantasies about medical omnipotence that neither doctor nor patient has a clear idea of the limits of medical science.

A life without limits is a life dominated by obsession. The obsession with cheating death has turned our pursuit of health into a sickness. The impact of simple lifestyle changes on our overall health has increased, not diminished, our anxieties. Ironically, we have become more susceptible than ever to our fears.

Obsessive Rituals of Salvation

"Obsession" is a word that both titillates and mystifies. Webster defines obsession as "a persistent disturbing preoccupation with an often unreasonable idea or feeling." My brush with the reality of obsession came when I was asked to testify as an expert witness in the endless legal wranglings over the disposition of the estate of Howard Hughes.

Howard Hughes was haunted by an overriding fear of disease. To protect himself, he developed compulsive rituals (the typical defense mechanism of the obsessed). Compulsive rituals are intended to appease powerful, feared forces and thereby ward off harm. To the nonobsessed, Hughes's ritual use of tissues when holding an object others had touched and his insistence that his staff wash their hands to protect him against germs (thirty, forty, even one hundred times a day) appear eccentric, at best; but Hughes felt safe by using these rituals.

Today, some people are obsessed with diet in the way Howard Hughes was obsessed with germs, and their rituals

10

around diet are every bit as elaborate as his were around the agents of disease. They have special lists of "yes" foods and "no" foods to be ritually included in or excluded from the diet. Foods on the "no" list may include red meat, liver and other organ meats, eggs, whole milk, and butter. The foods on the "yes" list may include so-called miracle foods that are reputed to prevent disease: cruciferous vegetables and soy protein to prevent cancer; fruit and other sources of soluble fiber to prevent diabetes, high cholesterol, obesity, and colon cancer; and fish to prevent heart disease.

The irony of this ritual inclusion or exclusion of dietary items is that, despite the fervor with which experts promote these foods, we do not know whether the recommendations are sound or valid. Each new miracle food quickly becomes a marketing tool. Oat bran, for example, made the yes list for its supposed virtues in lowering cholesterol levels; it became a magical additive to everything from breakfast cereal to pizza dough. By the time researchers recognized that oat bran was of little value unless someone was already eating a low-fat diet, the concept of oat bran as a miracle food had become so entrenched that the truth had little effect on consumption.

The obsessive ritual of eating oat bran continues in spite of its low value because the tyranny of the dietary expert is no different from the tyranny of the medical expert. By and large, people assume the experts have their best interests at heart, but under close scrutiny, a self-serving motive appears. For example, in 1992 a study that praised walnuts as a positive factor in fighting heart disease became suspect because its sole support came from the California Walnut Commission.

Another obsessive ritual is the "health screening." This differs from a physical exam in that, although a physical exam is more thorough, a health screening is more focused

11

on function, whereas the physical exam rules out the presence or absence of disease. A health screening includes the amount of body fat, cholesterol level, muscle functions, and stress test outcome. Many people track their cholesterol level as if it were a passing or failing mark. Other pass/fail marks are earned for weight, number of hours of exercise per week, and a measurement called percentage of body fat.

Many religions hold that, at death, people make an accounting of their lives, weighing good deeds against bad deeds on a giant scale. With today's promise of longevity, some people act as if death itself is a judgment on them for imperfect living. They obsess about cholesterol, exercise, weight, and body-fat percentages in an effort to ward off that judgment. The irony is that no court of appeals exists to which we can bring our case when, despite our high marks, death inevitably asserts its dominion over us.

In such an obsessive atmosphere of worry and ritual, it is little wonder that people can be seduced by promises of longevity and grow dependent on the security offered by authority figures, the experts.

Dangers of Dependency

Dependency is a familiar state. We are born dependent, but nature tries not to let us stay dependent. However, like Odysseus, we are in constant danger of being seduced and betrayed. Luckily, we come into the world fortified by an ancient and priceless protective force called the instinct of self-preservation, and our very lives depend on our independence and our right to question and choose. But when we stay dependent too long, we undermine our natural instinct for self-preservation. Like an addiction, dependency eventually makes us fragile and impotent.

Consider the message of the mammography ad: a woman is safer with mammography than with breast self-examination. Most people don't see the implication of dependency in the message, because they believe that modern technology offers them foolproof protection against what they fear—death and dying. We might expect to be bamboozled by commercial advertisers but not by the medical advertisers.

Nowhere in the mammography ad does it say that there is a surplus of underutilized mammography units in the United States. With few patients to examine, mammographic technicians at these units fail to develop the skill and experience needed to administer the exams properly. Do the hospital's technicians featured in the ad know how to perform a mammogram properly? Is the miracle technology of a mammogram always correct? There is no way of telling. Some women who rely on mammography may get false security from the exam.

For example, as early as 1978, the National Cancer Institute revealed that it funded a program that inadvertently resulted in fifty-eight needless mastectomies. The dosages of X ray to which women were exposed who participated in a government-funded breast cancer screening program were thought to have actually created tiny tumors.

The mammography ad is not an isolated instance in which medical science promises certainty. Consider the case of fat in the diet. According to a recent Gallup poll, over 85 percent of the population knows that too much saturated fat can lead to heart disease. Over 50 percent say they have completely replaced butter in their diets with polyunsaturated substitutes such as margarine.

Is this a triumph of health education or the harbinger of new problems? Some researchers now suggests that too

13

much polyunsaturated fat may be linked to breast cancer and other diseases. By placing butter on the "no" list of foods, the "fats police" may have gone too far.

Consider the case of cholesterol. Many parents have tried to start their children on the right path to cardiac health by eliminating cholesterol-rich foods from their children's diets. Some researchers, however, suggest that lower cholesterol levels in children and young people are associated with higher levels of aggressiveness and an increased mortality rate from accidents and suicides.

Again we are in danger if we don't see the whole picture. Although lower cholesterol levels do reduce the risk of heart disease, they do not reduce overall mortality among people on cholesterol-lowering drugs or diet regimens. Even with low cholesterol levels people die of other causes, such as accidents or suicides. Which risk is greater: A high cholesterol level or dying in an accident? And even more to the point, how do we know that the assessment of risk won't change while we're pondering the dilemma?

What Does Medicine Really Know about Risk?

Risk is a concept central to the power of the medical experts. They want to reduce our "risk" of illness. But we have to ask, on what basis do they establish the risk associated with any behavior? Consider the concern over cancer risk.

Biochemist Bruce Ames, who developed the widely used Ames Test to determine whether particular environmental chemicals increase the risk of cancer, has repudiated the conclusions of much of his earlier research. Ames now believes that one of the standard ways of testing carcinogenicity—giving rats megadoses of the substance in question (called the maximum tolerated dose or MTD)—ignores the fact that the body's reaction to a substance depends on the dosage taken in.

The body is efficient at neutralizing small doses of carcinogens and other toxins, but it becomes overwhelmed when large quantities are introduced all at once. Megadoses may approximate the amount taken into the body over the course of a year or so, but ingesting a year's dose in an hour invalidates the test and overstates the risk of cancer.

Ames believes that MTD tests could label as lethal over half of all chemicals, whether natural or manufactured. The newly founded panel on risk at the National Academy of Sciences agrees in principle with his assessment. As an example of the excesses that can result when MTD testing is the primary method of determining risk, consider the case of dioxin, the chemical in Agent Orange.

Dioxin was once pronounced "the most dangerous substance on the face of the earth." Yet dioxin now appears to be less dangerous than was previously thought. Reinterpretation of the original animal studies shows that the danger was overestimated. And the only study to definitively link dioxin to excess cancer deaths found a slightly increased risk among 1,500 workers who had been exposed to 500 times the federally designated acceptable level—the highest exposure level in history. No increased risk of cancer was found in the same study among 3,500 workers who received an average of 90 times the acceptable level of exposure.

Sometimes risk is merely an artifact of our methods of assessment. Consider the case of human papillomavirus, suspected as a cause of cervical cancer because the virus has been found in some women (11.5 percent) who develop the disease. Recently, a new, more sensitive screening proce-

15

dure has found the human papillomavirus in 46 percent of women in routine gynecological testing.

Researchers may now have to rethink their ideas about risk involving the virus and cervical cancer, since far more women who do not get cancer carry the virus than women who do get cancer. It appears the risk of getting cervical cancer from human papillomavirus went down when better testing was developed. That's the tyranny!

What Medical Miracles?

While medical researchers are sometimes poor at assessing relative risk, they are suspiciously self-congratulatory in assessing their successes. One of the most pervasive misconceptions of the twentieth century is that advances in medical science have made the greatest difference in the quality of our general health.

In 1900 the death rate from tuberculosis was 200 per 100,000 Americans. By the 1950s, when the first effective antituberculosis drugs became available, the rate had *already* declined by 90 percent to 20 per 100,000. The decline was caused primarily by better nutrition and less crowding, not by advances in medical care.

A more recent example is the vast improvement in the U.S. death rate from heart disease. According to *Healthy People 2000,* the death rate dropped by a whopping 51 percent over the past twenty years. Today, heart disease is no longer the number-one cause of death for adults between the ages of thirty-five and sixty-five. But almost all the improvement can be attributed to simple lifestyle changes, not to changes in medical care. Bypass surgery and other medical interventions such as angioplasty, pacemakers, and so on to treat heart disease can make people feel better and live more productive lives, but there is no evidence to show that they increase the length of a person's life.

We are pretty knowledgeable when it comes to the quality of our health, and we know when we are not doing well. Each of us has our own "doctor within" that is almost invariably the best guide to assessing individual risk and promoting our health. All we need to do is learn to listen. This inner doctor does simple things like telling us what foods to eat, how long we should sleep, and so forth. For example, when one of my colleagues had hepatitis and did not know it, her body shunned all oils and chocolate and begged for tomatoes and bananas, which had nutrients that she needed.

According to a study from Yale Medical School, a person's answer to the simple question, "Is your health excellent, good, fair, or poor?" is a better predictor of who will live or die over the next decade than is a rigorous physical examination. Older people in the study who said their health was "poor" were seven times more likely to die in the next twelve years than those who said their health was "excellent"—even when physical examinations showed both groups were in comparable health. As a matter of fact, almost no result from a thorough physical exam showed any relation to how long a person lived over the next twelve years.

The doctor within may be a carryover from our ancestral biology. Ecologists have noted for decades that many animals use medicinal plants and herbs to treat their ailments, perhaps even practicing preventive medicine. Many of these herbs and plants are also eaten by humans for similar purposes. Rhesus monkeys in Nepal, for example, eat dirt that contains a high concentration of kaolinite, formerly used as the active ingredient in the antidiarrheal medicine

Kaopectate. Pregnant women have been found in West Africa as well as Holmes County, Mississippi, who eat the same kind of dirt to settle their stomachs. Bears macerate the herb *Ligusticum porteri* and rub it on their paws and fur to benefit from the herb's apparent value as an insecticide and antiparasitic agent. Several American Indian tribes use the herb for the same purposes.

The doctor within is the source of cure even when medical intervention takes place. Even the simplest wound heals largely because of factors the medical experts cannot control and do not even understand.

What Is Health?

The World Health Organization defines health as the absence of disease. Although I am a physician, I'm not sure, nor are my colleagues, of what "health" means. For example, if health were equated with longevity, we should feel like the healthiest people in the world. A baby born in the United States today can expect to live 74.7 years. When its great-grandparents were born in 1900, they had a life expectancy of just 47.3 years. However, despite this objective evidence of improved health, a national poll taken in the mid-1980s found that only 55 percent of people surveyed were satisfied with their health, down from 61 percent ten years earlier.

Paradoxically, illness itself may sometimes be a peculiar form of health. I recall one patient of mine, a married woman, who felt that she could not develop her professional skills and self-esteem while married. She was prepared to divorce her husband and go her separate way. A subsequent serious illness almost killed her and left her with residual symptoms that limited her freedom of action and

18

altered her attitude about marriage and professional life. The illness and residual limitations allowed her within her marriage to successfully develop professional skills of excellence.

"Health" may bring its own form of illness. In my work at Massachusetts General Hospital, I became the psychiatric evaluator of patients with Parkinson's disease who were undergoing chemopallidotomy, injecting a chemical in the brain to kill cells that cause tremors. The procedure was experimental, and my job was to perform preoperative and postoperative psychiatric evaluations of patients undergoing the procedure.

One patient, a Canadian pediatrician in his fifties, was seriously embarrassed by his tremor. Although his hands shook all the time, he nonetheless continued to practice and function. Despite my recommendation against his suitability for the study, the procedure was performed.

When the man returned for a six-month post-op evaluation, the neurosurgeons were ecstatic: the patient was tremor-free. The psychiatric evaluation, however, revealed a less sanguine outcome. The tremor was gone, but so was the man's ability to function. He had become severely depressed, abandoned his pediatric practice, was suicidal, and needed constant nursing care and attention. His return to health—narrowly defined as freedom from the symptoms of a disease—had in fact rendered him incapable of leading a normal life.

Health may even be redefined before our eyes. I vividly recall the flippant attitude of a colleague who was lecturing on preventive treatment for people with diastolic blood pressure between 80 and 90 (90 is considered borderline or mild hypertension). The physician recommended more physician visits and more in-office blood-pressure monitoring for borderline-normal patients. The physician was un-

19

fazed by the fact that he was espousing a significant expansion of the "worried well."

When it was pointed out to him that his position would involve a large number of people, he replied, "True, this is a lot of people to watch, but I don't think it will overburden our health care system. Projections show a surplus of physicians in the next 10 years. This will give them something to do." Letting the medical experts control the definition of health is like putting the fox in charge of the henhouse.

Consider the "free assessments" offered by many purveyors of elective medical care: alcoholism treatment facilities, cosmetic surgeons, dermatologists. Does anyone have any statistics on the number of people being assessed as "not in need of our services?" I doubt it. In the alcoholism treatment field, for example, the assessment credo is extremely self-serving: if you think you might have an alcohol problem, you do. What usually gets assessed thoroughly, however, is the potential patient's ability to pay.

Retaining Our Independence

Even when people are wooed by the powerful emotional appeal of advertisements like the one I described at the beginning of this chapter, they can resist the urge to become dependent and childlike. An excellent place to start in trying to access the credibility of ubiquitous health warnings follows. Marcia Angell, M.D., executive editor of the *New England Journal of Medicine*, proposes some commonsense guidelines to help people sort out which health warnings should be heeded and which ignored:

1. *Ask whether what you are advised to do, or to avoid, is thought to have a big effect or a small one on the risk of*

getting the disease in question. For example, smokers are many times more likely to get lung cancer than nonsmokers, but women who take estrogens to prevent heart disease and osteoporosis after menopause are only slightly more likely to get breast cancer than women who don't take estrogens.

2. *Ask how common the disease is that the advice is meant to prevent. If it is very rare, even an important risk factor may not present much of a threat.* A statement that something doubles the risk of a disease is meaningless unless you know how common the disease is.

3. *Ask how strong the evidence is on which the advice is based.* If the advice is based on a single scientific study, especially a small one, wait to see whether later studies confirm it.

Along with these guidelines, the best advice is to use common sense and listen to the doctor within. If reducing your weight to that number found in the standard height-weight chart makes you irritable, fatigued, and guilty about what and when you eat, perhaps the guidelines in the tables are not right for you.

Despite all our research, all our knowledge, and all our technology, life and death are still a gamble. Some people will do everything right and die young; others will do everything wrong and live long, healthy lives. Adele Davis, the first proponent of "miracle foods," died of cancer in her fifties; Robert Rodale, founder of the health-oriented Rodale Press and of the popular bible of the wellness movement, *Prevention* magazine, died of heart disease at sixty.

Yet Winston Churchill, an obese, cigar-smoking, hard-drinking, meat-eating workaholic, lived to age ninety-one with his faculties and his physical stamina intact. Dr. William Castelli, the cholesterol expert who conducted the well-known Framingham study on heart-disease risk, says, "A third of the population doesn't get sick even if they do everything wrong."

Life and death remain mysteries. No one—not I, not the medical experts, not the people who write ads for mammography units—can offer us certainties, no matter how much we may long for them.

Chapter 2

Comfort of Conformity

> If one or both of your parents were alcoholics . . . *you* are still suffering, and you are not alone.
>
> —*Children of Alcoholism*

If the mysteries of the body ultimately elude the medical experts, how can anyone, whatever their professed expertise, claim greater dominion over the mind? An astonishing number of psychoexperts today—psychologists, psychiatrists, social workers, counselors, and a host of nonprofessionals who claim insight by virtue of having "been there"—believe they understand the human psyche and can fix whatever ails it.

The blurb above appears in large type on the back cover of a paperback handbook for adult children of alcoholic parents. Similar statements can be found in self-help books discussing behavioral disorders ranging from compulsive overeating to love addiction.

Messages like this one are the psychological Muzak of the 1990s: so commonplace, well-meaning, and benign-sounding that most of us neither pay attention to them nor take the time to consider their effect on us. But they are not benign. Like the mammography advertisement of chapter 1, these statements imply that we cannot trust our knowledge of ourselves. And like the mammography ad, they direct us toward experts as definitive sources of knowledge.

Most people find the mammography ad far more distasteful than this innocuous-sounding jacket blurb. But the jacket blurb—and the cultural force of psychoexpertise it represents—is far more insidious. It implies the removal of pain, the answers to questions, and a community of soulmates. It pushes a vulnerable button: the terrible longing for an all-powerful, all-knowing deliverer to offer protection from the uncertainty and lonely eminence of adulthood.

The life of a child, unlike that of an adult, is, for some people, the life of certainty and dependence. I remember crying myself to sleep many nights by imagining that my beloved father and mother were dead. Every morning when I awoke they were always there. When I was four, my parents took me to a farm where I had my first pony ride. As I sat confidently and proudly on that beautiful beast, I kept looking over at my folks for comfort and approval.

No matter what I tried, my mother and father were a source of support, comfort, and most important, a wall against loneliness. They really cared for me. Feeling that love and comfort, I could adjust to almost anything because I was not alone. Of course, like most children, I tested the limits of their love in many ways. But what I remember most is that I was not alone. Whatever the threat, whatever the situation, I could run back to safety.

As I grew older, other people began to come into my life. But new experiences and new people could never substitute for that original feeling of comfort and approval. Now as an adult, I provide the comfort. When I talk with my friends, listen to patients, hear my wife, sons, and grandchildren, I realize that I am alone. I am alone because

24

the wonderfully dependent, unique relation of child to parent no longer exists for me. I am the giver.

I substituted mentors for my father and mother. My wife and I are very close. I have a few friends and I can talk to my children. But, eminent and successful as I am, I still suffer the loneliness of being an adult. That loneliness makes many of us vulnerable to smart salespeople, organized paternalistic solutions, and the siren songs of experts who seem to have the answers. That solitude plays into the fantasies that occupy some adults' minds with hopes and desires to make what is gone come back. Some of us want the comfort of being a child again: protected, cared for, and not lonely.

That eternal desire for regression resides in us all. Differences surface in the ways we choose to express the desire. Some fulfill it by religious ritual. Others seek it in sexual fantasies and activities. Many others seek power, money, and fame. But quite often people seek the lost security and certainty of youth in illness or behavioral disorders.

Stress-Induced Compulsions

Millions of Americans today freely admit they suffer from a behavioral disorder. In fact, it is uncommon today to meet someone who doesn't identify himself or herself as afflicted with a compulsive behavior that is hurtful to themselves or others. I contrast this easy identification with the early days of the National Institute on Alcohol Abuse and Alcoholism, just two and a half decades ago, when my staff and I almost failed to find a well-known person to come forward and speak for our cause—to admit that he or she was an alcoholic person. They felt the risk of professional and personal reprisal was simply too great.

Behavioral disorders include alcoholism, drug addiction, compulsive gambling, overworking, overeating, compulsive sexual activity, premenstrual syndrome (PMS), posttraumatic stress disorder (PTSD), and other similar afflictions. The statistics that describe the prevalence of these problems are staggering.

According to estimates, twelve million Americans are drug addicts; twenty million are alcoholic; twenty-eight million are adult children of alcoholic people; thirty million suffer from anorexia or bulimia; forty million are codependent family members of alcoholic people or drug addicts; forty million are sex or love addicts; fifty million are compulsive overeaters, and fifty million women suffer from PMS. It is estimated that 96 percent of families are dysfunctional.

Although these figures are likely to be inflated, I believe they ring true in a wider sense. When people all around us are willing, even eager, to volunteer that they aren't coping well with their lives, there's clearly something awry on a large scale. Behavioral disorders are symptoms of extreme stress: the manifestations of gnawing physical or emotional pain, enormous financial and social pressures, boring lives, and deadening jobs that provide no opportunities for creativity and self-expression, and societal change so rapid that people cannot keep up with it.

Stress is not new to our times. A wave of what was called "neurasthenia" or "American nervousness," for example, swept the United States from 1880 to about 1920. Neurasthenia is defined as nervous exhaustion characterized by abnormal fatigability. It is also a catchall name for a group of symptoms affecting almost any part of the body. The symptoms are believed to be psychological and include a marked tendency to fatigue, lack of energy, back pain, memory loss, insomnia, depression, constipation, loss of appetite, and other varied symptoms. The condition was not as democratic as our present-day behavioral illnesses, however.

Neurasthenia mainly afflicted "brain-workers": the industrialists, managers, financiers, writers, artists, and intellectuals of the new middle class, along with their spouses. The neurasthenics, like the behaviorally ill of today, were caught on the cusp of a rapidly changing society. The symptoms and course of neurasthenia mirror the symptoms and course of those afflicted with behavioral problems.

In the past, when the stress of everyday living became intense and the uncertainty of life difficult to bear, people were able to find comfort and support in their communities. In their churches, extended families, or neighborhoods, they could identify with and find security in strong bonds with people similar to themselves. Today, the ready solace of family and church may be unavailable, and the lack of stable communities may explain the powerful need for twelve-step support groups.

Without effective support systems, people are likely to seek artificial stimulation to alter their reality: to help them relax and feel alive and important, and to relieve physical or emotional pain. Such stimulation is precisely what a behavioral disorder provides, whether the object of the person's compulsion is alcohol, sex, cocaine, gambling, or food. But the stimulant never fills the need. As the compulsion grows, the problem worsens, and the pain of the person's isolation deepens and becomes unbearable.

Identity by Diagnosis

Because compulsive behavior is a symptom of a deeper spiritual malaise, people with behavioral afflictions are vulnerable to the message reflected in the jacket blurb: "You are not alone." This message is the central assertion of most forms of therapy, counseling, and other care directed at the behaviorally afflicted. Even if the "cure" itself is mechanical—for example, carefully controlled nicotine withdrawal programs for smokers, or diet-and-exercise programs for compulsive eaters—it is often set within more elaborate structures such as group therapy, cathartic confessions, and trust-building activities such as wilderness encounter groups.

The price the behaviorally afflicted are asked to pay for their cure appears small: they must be willing to change their view of themselves from having a problem to being the problem. They must identify themselves with and by their problem. In return, they gain a new identity, one that no longer suffers from the hurt and isolation that manifested itself in the behavioral problem, but one that offers the comfort and security of belonging to a group with similar problems.

In psychiatric terms, identity is more than just a way of defining who we are: it structures our time, gives us specific goals to pursue, and tells us whom to spend time with. If we are alcohol/love/sex/food/drug/gambling/shopping/work addicts or victims of any other behavioral problem, we have an instant community (others like us), an instant purpose (to recover), and an instant structure for our lives (the program of recovery).

Most people, even those who have never known anyone with alcohol problems, are familiar with the Alcoholics Anonymous greeting: "Hi, I'm Jane, and I'm an alcoholic." The AA groups all over the world welcome anyone willing to make that assertion. If someone is willing to conform to this formula, the door is open: AA meetings are held on and off twenty-four hours a day in most cities, all of them offering instant, unconditional acceptance. The AA program is perhaps the closest we have come to what Marshall McLuhan saw as the evolving "global village," a world in which all have a common culture, and hence a sense of belonging, through the agency of mass communications. Instead of the global village, however, we have evolved global group therapy.

When Abnormality Is the Norm

Someone in existential pain does not have to look far to find a diagnosis with which to identify and a community of sufferers to join. It is not even necessary to have an identifiable behavioral problem to fall within the purview of diagnosis. Family members who are not themselves engaged in destructive behaviors can gain access if they are spouses, children, or even grandchildren of someone who has a problem.

Once someone identifies with a diagnosis, he or she never has to give it up. Books, seminars, AA-type groups, and treatment facilities continue to call people "recovering" or "survivors" if they have ever experienced problems. These open-ended terms effectively tie these people to their illness-identity long after the behaviors themselves have changed. Even those who do not yet see themselves as having a behavioral problem may be "ticking time bombs"—because they were exposed to traumatic events, such as a parent's alcoholism, which the experts say will inevitably lead to problems.

The physician-author of a popular self-help guide to "healing the child within" takes these diagnostic criteria to their outer limits. He estimates that "80 to 95% of people did not receive the love, guidance and other nurturing necessary to form consistently healthy relationships, and to feel good about themselves and what they do."

It would be easy to impugn the motives of this physician for making such a broad statement unsupported by research or objective findings. Statistically, of course, his point is nonsense: the norm cannot consist of 5 to 15 percent of a population. Yet in a broader sense, his figures represent a kind of truth. The figures epitomize a mammoth sense of loss, an inexplicable sense of sadness, and an insupportable sense of guilt. I can believe that most of us would like to consider ourselves wounded so we can offer ourselves up for healing.

Urge to Merge

By accepting ourselves as sick, we enter a powerfully attractive world where we can lose our exhausting individuality and the horror of reality. In this world, all-knowing, all-powerful, and all-kind beings promise solace, companionship, and unconditional acceptance. We experience the bliss of merging—with a therapist, or a group, or a recovery program.

It is no surprise that many of the behavioral therapies today talk about an "inner child" who must be nurtured and healed. In fact, what these treatments offer is an opportunity for regression to an infantile state—dependent and comforted by the security found in the answers and acceptance of experts.

Treatment rituals—talking to a therapist once a week or studying the twelve steps and twelve traditions of AA— provide solace for the child in us. They offer order, comfort, and companionship in a chaotic and lonely world. Like the rituals of the medical profession, they bring back to some people the comforting memories of their childhood days when their parents were providers and protectors.

What's more, these rituals allow participants to remain self-absorbed. In AA meetings, for example, people retell their stories without interruption or comment from others. The participants are encouraged to see the similarities, not the differences, in their experiences. Everything in the world becomes an extension of the self; it is a re-creation of the original omnipotent fantasy of infancy.

The twelve steps of AA have become the model for many other forms of treatment and self-help today. And it is no wonder. The twelve steps contain some of the most powerful comforts currently available. The idea that there are a specific number of steps to follow to attain happiness is a powerful notion, reminiscent of once-powerful but now culturally inert prescriptions, such as the Ten Commandments.

The content of the twelve steps is similarly soothing. The fundamental tenet of AA, for example, asserts that people are powerless over alcohol. In twelve-step spin-offs, the overpowering problem may be food, sex, gambling, or other compulsions. This sense of powerlessness is very consoling, because it releases people from a sense of responsibility. The idea that the misfortunes of life are in some way connected to an addiction or compulsion also serves to keep people from having to face reality—the shortness of life and the seeming insignificance of each of us.

If addiction is the root of all evils, then one can conclude that there is no unmotivated suffering, and there are no inexplicable accidents. There is no such thing as chance or fate. All things originate from our behavior and in that way a certain amount of certainty is bestowed upon the uncertain.

In this context, it is no surprise that a steady stream

of information about addiction and recovery dominates television talk shows and paperback books. The mass media market thrives when it offers neatly packaged products that touch a deep emotional chord.

Freedom from Guilt

With a return to childhood through confession, identification, and surrender comes a return to original innocence. In the fourteenth and fifteenth centuries, wandering pardoners assuaged people's sense of guilt by selling them worthless pieces of paper that granted expiation for their earthly sins. Today's pardoners are the authors and therapists who grant similar exculpation by a diagnosis of compulsive or obsessive behavior.

It's a commonly held belief that none of us would do wrong—commit a crime, flout the law, cheat on a spouse, perjure ourselves—except under the influence of an overwhelming compulsion. Marion Barry, for example, the mayor of Washington, D.C., who was caught in a police sting smoking crack cocaine, repeatedly blamed his womanizing, lying, and drug use on alcoholism. He is only one in a long line of public officials to beat their breasts in public, claiming exculpation because of an overpowering compulsion.

The idea that people who have been maltreated will inevitably maltreat others is another way of freeing people from guilt and responsibility. During a highly publicized trial, Joel Steinberg was tried for beating his adopted daughter, Lisa, to death while his common-law wife, Hedda Nussbaum, did nothing to stop it. People debated whether Nussbaum should be held legally responsible as an accomplice to the killing.

She was not tried, largely because Steinberg abused her so flagrantly that no one believed she could have crossed him to get help for the child. But many were troubled by this decision because the crime was so brutal and the hours of the child's suffering so long that few could imagine how any human being, even one severely brutalized as Hedda Nussbaum was, could have felt so little responsibility.

We model our behavior on those who raise and care for us, and so if we are abused and feel powerless we come to associate power with the abusive behavior and even emulate it in our fantasy lives. But there's a chasm between fantasy and reality. Plenty of people abused as children do not beat their own children. It is not a case of all or nothing.

As a psychiatrist, I know that people do sometimes suffer unduly with a burden from the past, but I have never seen anyone free himself or herself from the past by using the burden as a scapegoat. One of my first alcoholic patients reported that when she was born, her mother abandoned her in a toilet. Although the mother later reclaimed her, the patient always felt she was "a piece of shit"—worthless, lifeless, stinking, discarded. She believed that anyone who cared for her also became, by association, a worthless piece of shit, whom she then discarded.

In treatment, she would do well for a short time, then revert to her previous patterns. A year after she failed to return to me for further treatment, I heard that she had killed herself with a combination of sleeping pills and alcohol.

This woman believed in the model of a "normal" mother-child relationship preferred by the experts and accepted by society. Because her experience did not match the model, she believed she was worthless, and that all of her problems and sorrows were inevitably connected to her "abnormal" relationship. Was she a lifelong victim of her mother's abandonment? Or was she the victim who focused on destructive memories, holding herself back from getting well because she feared to take responsibility for her life?

In this respect, I believe our obsession with compulsions, and with treatment for compulsions, is dangerous and counterproductive. We regress to childhood, while the adult world continues to make adult demands on us. We become obsessed with the past, while minute by minute, the present drains away and the future is lost.

Does Treatment Work?

It might be possible to accept some of the ambiguities of treating people for behavioral problems if treatment worked. In spite of society's huge investment to treat behavioral problems, there is little evidence that shows treatment works for behavioral problems, and plenty of evidence to show it does not.

For behavioral problems and emotional problems, treatment is probably an expensive luxury. The classic demonstration of this fact is found in a widely quoted study by the Kaiser Foundation Hospital in Oakland, California. The hospital evaluated 150 patients for psychotherapy, but was unable to accommodate 23 of them immediately and placed them on a waiting list. At the end of six months, the 23 on the waiting list were reevaluated, as were the members of the original group of 150 who had already received six months of therapy. The 23 people on the waiting list were doing as well or better than the 127 people in therapy.

The weight-loss industry is a multibillion dollar business, but 95 percent of people treated in its programs gain no permanent benefits. At the same time, people who lose weight on their own, finding their own formulas and making them work for them, are permanently successful nearly two-thirds of the time.

The alcohol and drug treatment industry will admit that its treatments have a long-term failure rate of at least 50 percent. Yet studies suggest that most people who recover from alcohol and drug problems do so on their own. Even people who decide to break their addiction to the alleged most addictive drug of all—nicotine—are successful nearly 95 percent of the time when they do so on their own.

Without questioning why their treatments usually lead to failure and why self-treatment usually leads to success, the alcohol and drug treatment industries devise "new and improved" therapies. The latest example of this phenomenon is called "relapse prevention"—in effect, a way to get patients to pay for the failures of the treatment process.

As happens with behavioral problems of all kinds, including addictions, time is a far more likely healer than treatment. Even among people addicted to drugs or alcohol, clinicians are well aware of a phenomenon called "maturing out." Maturing out means the tendency for most people to get over their addictions or destructive behaviors as they get older. Even long-term heroin addicts, whom people believe to be the least amenable to treatment, show the same tendency to mature out. Over two-thirds of heroin addicts mature out of their addiction.

One of the variables that we cannot measure as we examine the maturing-out phenomenon is the impact of the self-fulfilling prophecy, that is, telling people they can't break their addiction without help.

Sometimes treatment or other interventions may actually do harm. A recent study reported in the *Journal of the American Medical Association* warned that suicide prevention programs stir up young people's depressed feelings and contribute to romanticizing suicidal behavior. Suicide is

35

currently the third-leading cause of death among young people aged fifteen to twenty-four.

The mystification surrounding mental health treatment keeps people from asking for accountability from treatment providers. When treatment fails, people usually find fault with themselves—the "damaged" or uncertain party—or with external factors, rather than with the treatment provider—the expert who supposedly has all of the answers.

I recall a colleague who related to me the story of a psychiatric hospital that responded to a rash of suicides among local youth by holding a press conference to educate the public. The director spent most of the time discussing the hospital's methods of working with suicidal young people. When someone in the audience pointed out that one of the recent victims had been treated at the hospital, the psychiatrist responded, "That just demonstrates how difficult a problem we're dealing with."

What about the Truly Mentally Ill?

The areas where experts and their advice are needed the most are often the areas where they are offered the least. Although many people with problems of adjustment, discontent, and lack of self-esteem are treated expensively and unsuccessfully, people with authentic and pressing needs—the chronically mentally ill—are often left literally out in the cold. The chronically mentally ill make up a significant percentage of the homeless population living on grates and under bridges in every major city. Not only is there no money to bring these people indoors, but in the process of deinstitutionalizing the mentally ill, the psychiatric and long-term-care hospitals that formerly treated them have largely been dismantled.

The idealistic goal of deinstitutionalization was to give chronically mentally ill people, who could be managed by medication, the right to live as part of the general community. But the reality is that the system simply thrust these people out on their own, with little effective supervision and little social support. Not surprisingly, many threw away their medicine, particularly since psychoactive drugs often have unpleasant side effects. It still amazes me to realize that a mental health establishment that urges once-a-day support-group meetings for people who overeat, gamble, or drink alcohol would abandon the population of chronically mentally ill people who survive with so little day-to-day support.

The more the definition of alcoholism was broadened to include anyone who has a problem with alcohol, the more the people whose lives are destroyed by alcoholism are shunted aside. As the definition of any problem is expanded, resources are diluted. The field then focuses its efforts on those people who appear to have the greatest chance of succeeding in treatment. No matter that these are the very people who will most likely get better on their own.

An inverted triangle illustrates the pattern for use of resources in most mental hospitals. Those who needed the most got the least; those who needed the least got the most. The largest share of resources went to maintain the administrative and managerial staff. Only a minuscule portion trickled its way down to the patients. The prevailing fantasy about resources was that there were always more to go around, that the director's perquisites did not affect the money available for patient care, and that the resources devoted to people who will get better on their own did not compromise the care of people who truly require help.

When the Search for Health Becomes Sickness

Just as society's resources may be misdirected by following experts' advice on an impossible quest, so too may our personal resources be vastly misdirected if we use our flaws to define our way into a comforting identity-by-diagnosis lifestyle. The course of a life can be changed by defining behavior as a problem.

For example, a twenty-five-year-old woman experiencing a vulnerable and lonely time in her life decided to join an AA group that a coworker belonged to. This woman showed none of the clinical signs of alcoholism and was not even a particularly frequent drinker. However, she had become frightened by several episodes of excessive drinking during the breakup of a stormy marriage. Having lost her friends and her social support system when her marriage ended, she became an active AA proponent and quickly built a new life around the AA group.

Instead of maturing out of her alcohol problem, which seemed to be a temporary one related to her divorce, six years later she continued to spend several evenings a week at AA and other twelve-step meetings. She believed she was in danger of losing all the progress she had made, although she had not had a drinking episode in all those years.

There is nothing wrong with this woman's choice of an AA group for support. Perhaps she gained something from choosing the group to work out a personal problem. But in the process she lost her individual identity and sense of responsibility by devoting so much of her energy to recovery, and by defining herself as permanently sick. Could she have gained more and lost less if there were another way for her to cope with the dislocation she felt after her divorce? Maybe.

Without a definition of normal, how can those who

purport to be experts differentiate between instances where treatment for a behavioral problem is needed, and instances in which the behavioral problem is merely a symptom of a temporary crisis?

Consider, for example, the case of Janet Frame, one of New Zealand's most respected modern novelists, who in the late 1940s was diagnosed schizophrenic chiefly because she could not overcome her extreme shyness and complete her training as a teacher. Her only real problem was that her behavior did not match the experts' model of how a teacher should behave.

During eight years in a mental hospital, she withdrew further and further into herself; as a result, she was labeled intractable, given shock treatments, and finally referred for a lobotomy. She escaped the knife, ironically, because once again she did not fit into what the experts offered as the normal model of a schizophrenic. Her physician accidentally learned that a book of her short stories had won a major literary prize and deduced from her achievement that she was an artist not a schizophrenic.

In the context of a socially valued achievement, Frame's odd behavior was reclassified "normal." Perhaps it *was* normal all along—a spiritual revolt by a gifted artist against a social system in which her only option was to subordinate her talents to her need to make a living.

I am not suggesting that the diagnosis of mental illness or other behavioral problems is merely a means of social control by experts, an idea made fashionable in the 1970s and 1980s by psychiatrist and author Thomas Szasz and others. As a psychiatrist, I have seen enough human suffering to know that there are people who are not normal, who are seriously mentally ill, and who pose a danger to themselves and others.

But how can we channel our resources to these people if

39

the professionals who provide services to them believe, as did the physician-author I mentioned earlier, that 80 to 95 percent of the population is in need of psychological treatment? That belief may be the single biggest obstacle to distinguishing mental illness from spiritual malaise and treating each appropriately.

Must You Conform?

Psychiatry, psychology and the medical or social arts that depend on them have become devil's advocates and sorcerers' apprentices of conformity. . . . Of all betrayals, their treachery has been the greatest, for in them we have placed our remaining hope, and in them, sadly, hope has fled. Equating protest with madness and non-conformity with neurosis . . . they labor with art and skill to gut the flame that burns eternally at the core of being.

—Robert Lindner
Psychiatrist

Robert Lindner is best known for his book *Must You Conform?*, which inspired the James Dean classic movie *Rebel Without a Cause*. Today, largely because of mass-market psycho paperbacks and talk show psychoevangelism, the role of psychoexpertise in leading the mass of us—those of us who suffer spiritual wounds rather than mental ones—toward conformity has become far greater than Lindner could have imagined.

What was the price? How much creativity is lost in the painful and pointless quest to assign a diagnosis to every human idiosyncrasy and conform to the one "true" model offered by experts? My eldest son, who is a successful and respected journalist and author, was accepted into the premed program at Johns Hopkins University in Baltimore. Neither my wife nor I had attended an Ivy League school;

we were proud of our son and held great expectations for his medical career.

We had a picture in our minds of how an Ivy League student should look and behave: the proper young gentleman with all the right clothes and manners. The model offered to us of the Ivy League student did not turn out to be our reality. My son was suspended early in his freshman year for perpetrating a crude prank. I was angry and upset with him, and I grew even angrier when I discovered he had told the college dean that I would brutalize him when I found out he was leaving school.

When I confronted him in his dormitory, he was irritatingly cheerful—he had already found himself a job in an advertising agency. He stopped me before I could get a word out and told me not to burden him with my feelings. Believe me, I have known parents who have committed their children in psychiatric hospitals for less reason.

I'm glad I didn't try to force him to conform to my wife's and my expectations. Somehow we were able to see that the prank was our son's way of asserting his individuality. He didn't want to be premed at Hopkins. But how was he to tell his parents who had lovingly endowed him with their hopes and dreams, believed strongly in the stereotypical model of the proper Ivy League student, and sent him off to school with all the right clothes and manners?

I've met others like my son who did not want to follow the prescribed path, but unlike him, could not sustain their rebellion. These people remain adolescents long into adulthood. For a time they embrace the definitions of acceptable behavior, then they channel their pent-up creativity into doing things to get out of situations they don't like, such as by performing spectacular pranks or engaging in self-destructive behaviors, such as getting fired or having an accident.

The last thing such people need is to embrace another

schema to conform to. The psychoexperts who write self-help books and create treatment programs assume that what all of us need most is to know that "we are not alone." The book jacket blurb at the beginning of this chapter says that we are not alone. And the subtitle of another popular self-help book tells us our crises are predictable. The goal of self-help books is to help people feel better about themselves: "When we don't fit in," writes a well-known psychologist, "we are likely to think of our behavior as evidence of our inadequacies."

But can a support peer group answer our primal need for self-expression and self-esteem whose loss is at the heart of so much malaise today? Or does a support peer group merely mask the deep despair, prolong the adolescent quest for self, and make the quest to "find oneself" a sacrament or a sickness—instead of a temporary failure of nerve?

In this search for self, it's no wonder that the self-help book market is largely a market of repeat buyers. It's no wonder that people go from therapist to EST to rolfing to primal scream to analysis to gestalt to transcendental meditation. In this endless quest people are looking for a key to their authentic selves. What they find instead is the siren song of conformity—a comforting but empty promise.

There's nothing wrong with wanting life not to hurt or not to be difficult. That desire tests the wellsprings of human ingenuity, and is the reason we have today's technologies along with our hopes and dreams for tomorrow. But if that desire leads us to succumb to our childlike yearning to depend on expert formulas and powerful outside forces for answers, we will be disappointed. We'll find ourselves mired in an endless adolescence, cut off from our innate will and power to change, trapped in the very pain that sent us looking for help, and robbed of the one gift that can redeem us: the sense of our own individuality and uniqueness.

Authentic Human Comfort

If the psychoexperts and their message of comforting conformity can't deliver peace of mind, then how can people plagued by inner turmoil, unwanted habits, repressed memories, or unresolved painful experiences achieve peace and comfort within themselves? The Danish philosopher Sören Kierkegaard believed happiness consists of three essential elements: something to do, someone to love, and something to hope for. When people have to do without those essentials, they fall prey to whatever avenues of escape that are offered. They become dependent on outside supports, even those of dubious value, for self-esteem and self-worth.

In contrast, people who have a stake in the world—a rewarding job, relations with family and friends, dreams and goals based on realistic possibilities—are less likely to lose faith with themselves and unlikely to define themselves by a diagnosis. A book, a support group, a workshop, a therapy session, or a course of psychoanalysis offers a temporary substitute for what gives life meaning. Instead of turning our attention endlessly inward and to the past, we would be better off turning our experiences outward and to the future.

It is easy to feel that the world is too complicated to be mastered by our own resources. With all the expertise being hawked everywhere, it is easy to feel that there must be a formula for happiness we haven't learned yet. The fact that there isn't may be a great disappointment. And since it turns the future back into our own hands, it may make us wonder uneasily if we are up to the responsibility.

I believe we are up to the responsibility, and I owe my belief in part to a former patient of mine, a nursing student at Massachusetts General Hospital, who was referred to me for treatment to aid her in completing her courses for graduation. Although this young woman showed up promptly and faithfully for each appointment, she did not seem particularly interested in her sessions with me. For two months I continued to treat her, despite the fact that I had no idea what she wanted from me or what possible good I could be doing for her.

Although she was planning to continue living in the Boston area, she terminated therapy with me immediately on receiving her nursing degree. Two or three weeks later, I saw in the paper that the man she married right after graduation had been killed in a freak accident on their honeymoon while fixing a flat tire. When I met her some weeks later and extended my condolences, I was taken aback by her reply: "At least I had him for two weeks." The response seemed so artificial and contrived that I felt even more guilty about my work with her. I obviously had not helped her with her problems or her response would have been less contrived and more human.

Five years later, after she had remarried and had her first child, she sent me one of the warmest letters I have ever received from a patient, thanking me for all I had done for her. At first, I was astounded. Then I began to realize that she had known better than I what she needed and had, in fact, gotten what she wanted while she was in therapy with me. She had turned to therapy because she was growing frightened as she came to the end of her student days, and I, as her psychiatrist, sat with her through that difficult time as she wrestled with her fears and grew into herself. My expertise did not help her—my humanity did.

We do not need expertise to give this gift of humanity to each other. When we are suffering from the pains of growing up, taking risks, recognizing ourselves as fallible and mortal, and accepting the mortality and fallibility of those who love us, we do not need formulas—and we certainly should beware of treatment that encourages an empty conformity.

We need what we humans have always needed: authentic contact with compassionate, caring, fellow human beings. Sometimes, that contact can be found in the realm of experts, but such generosity and love is usually found in our everyday lives. We are all in a position of offering basic humanity and civility as long as we believe we have this to give, and as long as we believe we are capable of giving it.

Chapter 3

The Experts' Greatest Victory

Study Finds Alcoholism Touches 4 in 10 in U.S. Health
& Human Services Secretary Sullivan Says Other Figures
Understate Problem
> —*Washington Post*, 1 October 1991

To judge by a headline quoting the nation's highest health
official, alcohol abuse problems in the United States in
1991 were out of control. Few of us questioned this
impression, and why should we? The nation's top health
expert offered statistics to back his claim. Even today, one
celebrity after another is going for alcoholism treatment at
well-known treatment centers, and the talk shows and
newspapers are filled with emotion-laden stories of alcohol-
related tragedies. With such an abundance of news, it
sounds like most people must be experiencing alcohol
problems. But this type of headline is seriously misleading.

The headline says a study shows that four of ten Americans are affected by alcoholism. There are things we need
to know, however, before we can understand what this
means. First, the method of collecting this type of data is
invariably faulty. The actual question to which the headline
refers was "Have you lived with, been related to or married
to a problem drinker or alcoholic?" The survey, conducted

47

by the National Center for Health Statistics, did not define either "alcoholic" or "problem drinker."

No time frame was given, so the person involved could have had alcohol problems two decades before and have successfully recovered. In addition, the survey did not define the term "related to"; the person in question could have been a distant relative, with no real impact on the interviewee's life. The method, language, and scaling used when conducting a survey is imperative to producing credible data. By asking questions in a certain way, experts can produce data that satisfy any hypothesis.

As we have seen, experts can prey on our most fundamental anxieties—death, aging, loneliness, fear, guilt, and lack of control. They can probe for our weaknesses and exploit our insecurities. Highly emotional and easily manipulated issues, such as alcohol use and abuse, attract expert attention. But alcohol abuse has a special meaning to tyrannous experts because it can be viewed as their greatest victory.

As a longtime student of humanity's relation with alcohol, I do believe that the United States has a bigger problem with alcoholism than many other countries—even countries that drink more, and more regularly, than our own. I also believe that the experts with headlines, like the one quoted above, are part of the problem.

The tendency of experts to describe alcoholism as a problem that is larger than life, out of control, and amenable only to the strongest public policy measures contributes to its bloated perception and to the prevalence of alcohol problems. Public fears about alcohol are used to justify stronger laws to punish offenders and more restrictions on the purchase of alcohol beverages. These very policies, however, victimize alcoholic people, create public policy solutions that don't work, and actually foster alcohol problems.

Alcohol as Irresistible Force

As stated above, experts focus their attention and manipulative efforts on emotionally laden subjects, and alcohol use stirs up as much emotion as the abortion issue—except that there is no pro-choice voice for alcohol. Although two-thirds of the adult American public drinks alcohol beverages at least occasionally, and the overwhelming majority never experiences any problems with their drinking, many people are made to feel guilty and fearful about alcohol use. Facts and issues have become so convoluted that people who abstain from alcohol, and even some who do not, believe alcohol is an irresistible agent of evil influence. When they hear of someone with alcohol problems, many drinkers secretly feel, "There but for the grace of God go I."

The strength of this fear of alcohol as manufactured by experts and their supporters is not a new phenomenon. It was expressed vividly in a radio broadcast by Prohibitionist preacher Billy Sunday in 1919, just before the Eighteenth Amendment took effect to prohibit the manufacture and sale of alcohol: "The reign of tears is over," he said. "The slums will soon be a memory. We will turn our prisons into factories and our jails into storehouses and corncribs. Men will walk upright now, women will smile and the children will laugh. Hell will forever be rent."

The strength of this message has been so pervasive that some people continue to harbor the secret belief that any use of alcohol is wrong. When Congress raised the excise taxes on alcohol beverages in 1990, for example, no one objected when commentators referred to the tax as a "sin tax." Not even alcohol-beverage manufacturers, who spend millions of dollars to advertise the virtues of their products, objected. Not even the treatment community, which fought long and hard to have alcoholism recognized as a disease instead of a moral failing, objected. As a result of this passive behavior, the alcoholism community of experts achieved a victory.

Control of Consumption

By the alcoholism community of experts I mean alcoholism researchers, treatment professionals, government bureaucrats, consumer advocates, and people who have had alcohol problems themselves and now devote their efforts to combating its use. Their biased and often self-righteous efforts strongly contribute to our societal beliefs in the overwhelming power and evil of alcohol. In a high-profile report entitled *Healthy People 2000*, the U.S. Department of Health and Human Services declared a goal of reducing by 25 percent the per capita consumption of alcohol by Americans fourteen and over by the year 2000.

The goal does not speak about people who drink too much. The rhetoric is clear. It says drinking by anyone. Inclusion of this goal as outright government health policy is another significant victory for those experts who believe alcohol is so dangerous that no one can safely drink.

These people, who include experts now at work in the alcoholism treatment and research fields, don't want an outright ban on alcohol use, as we had during Prohibition. They believe—and with good cause, since the Eighteenth Amendment was the only constitutional amendment ever repealed—that people would revolt against another Prohibition. Instead, they want to manipulate people into drinking less by making alcohol more difficult to buy. They want higher taxes on alcohol beverages, more restrictions on where and when alcohol beverages can be sold, and public education stressing the dangers of alcohol.

The experts' control-of-consumption theory is based on a mathematical model that reportedly shows as alcohol becomes more expensive, general consumption will decline and so will the incidence of heavy drinking and alcohol problems. This sounds like simple supply and demand theory, but there is no real-world evidence that this theory works, and there's plenty of commonsense evidence that it doesn't work.

My laboratory has been that of sick people, but I've observed that people on skid row somehow get the alcohol they need. Even Kitty Dukakis, sitting at the side of her husband the governor of Massachusetts, told of how she used products that contained alcohol to satisfy her need when alcoholic beverages were not available to her.

Unsubstantiated though the model is, control of consumption is not the thinking of some small extremist wing of the alcohol research and treatment community. It is the view held by one of the most prestigious organizations on alcohol abuse—the National Institute on Alcohol Abuse and Alcoholism (NIAAA). This is the federal agency I founded over twenty-five years ago to lead the nation's efforts against alcohol problems.

A style sheet published by the Office of Substance Abuse Prevention (OSAP), now called CSAP (Center for Substance Abuse Prevention) and a sister government organization to NIAAA, tells federal grantees they cannot use the term "responsible use" in any written materials about alcohol. Alcohol cannot be used responsibly, they say, because "there is risk associated with all use." In making the wickedness of alcohol a matter of government policy, the experts have bested the rest of us again.

If the alcohol experts who favor control of consumption are right, alcohol problems should be lower now than they were in the past. Annual American liquor consumption,

51

measured by tax receipts and industry reports, peaked at 2.76 gallons of pure alcohol per person in 1980 and 1981 and has sharply declined since then. By 1987, according to NIAAA, consumption had dropped to 2.54 gallons, the lowest since 1970. Yet the number of alcohol problems are reported as rising.

Although the methods and theories spouted by experts seem convincing and logical, the truth of the matter, or the long-term results, is usually quite different. We need to be less awed by theory and philosophy and more inclined to search for our own answers.

Corporate Guilt

The experts have won another battle in the arena of alcohol: even the manufacturers of alcohol beverages share some of the collective American guilt and shame perpetuated by those who view alcohol and its distributors as purveyors of harm or evil. This ambivalence about alcohol puts them in the complex position of selling products they believe, on some level, to be bad for those who buy them.

The experts' manipulation of the industry's guilt and ambivalence about its products keeps it operating like a classic neurotic, always working against its own best interests. For example, many manufacturers are now diversifying into nonalcohol beers and wines. I believe this move reinforces the idea that something is inherently wrong with what has been taken out of the product, just as beverage cans labeled "caffeine free" and "saccharin free" reinforce the idea that caffeine and saccharin are harmful substances. Advertising that uses tag lines such as "keep your edge" reinforces consumers' fear of losing control, intensifies their guilt about alcohol, and plays into the experts' strategy.

It appears to me that the pervasive guilt and doubt manufactured by alcohol experts in the alcohol-beverage industry has resulted in failed attempts to create a credible set of assumptions about alcohol abuse and alcoholism. For instance, the industry to this day resists calling alcohol a drug. Like many individuals, the industry treats "drug" as a bad word. A drug is simply a substance that affects the body. By that definition, alcohol is certainly a drug. But the popular connotation, fed by not-so-subtle associations to illegal drugs, makes the word "drug" dirty and demeaning.

The alcohol-beverage industry continually plays into the hands of the social forces that both oppose its business activities and promote guilt about alcohol use. The industry, for example, provides just lukewarm and inconsistent support for the concept of responsible drinking. Some people in the industry are attracted to the disease model of alcoholism because they feel it exonerates alcohol as the cause of alcoholism. According to the disease model of alcoholism, certain drinkers, perhaps by genetic or familial predisposition, are strongly susceptible to alcoholism.

The predicament for the industry arises when disease-model proponents conclude that, since susceptibility to alcoholism is not easily determined, there is no way of being sure who will become an alcoholic. Thus, the disease advocates claim that lowering availability and controlling consumption are the best prevention techniques. And that is precisely what the industry's opponents are planning to do. Such techniques mirror the thinking of the antismoking groups that believe young people and adults are a susceptible lot who can be seduced to smoke and addiction.

The tyranny of alcohol experts does not end with the issue of availability. Similarly, when the antialcohol advocates try to ban alcohol advertising by claiming it encourages people to drink, the industry makes the case that advertising may lead a person to choose one brand over the other but will not cause someone to make the decision to drink. I agree that all available worldwide research supports the industry's position on the issue of advertising. The industry weakens its position, however, when it points out how many ads it pays for trying to prevent drunk driving and underage drinking. People and industries can't have it both ways.

Experts are able to tyrannize people who are afraid to speak out and stand up for their own opinions and beliefs. Being defensive doesn't help the industry either. They play it safe because they never forget that Prohibition once put them out of business—the only U.S. constitutional amendment enacted that banned an industry's product and then was repealed.

They rightly fear a return of Prohibition, but prohibition in an updated form: product liability lawsuits. One alcohol-beverage company executive told me that he and his colleagues were purging their files of all references to alcohol as beneficial. They feared that such statements could be used against them in court to make them liable in lawsuits about alcohol-related accidents.

If the people who are most affected by the tyranny of the alcohol experts do not fight for the integrity of their product, why should the rest of society?

Guilt and Drunk Driving Policies

Blaming advertising and alcohol for many social ills encourages bizarre and counterproductive public policies. In the early 1980s, for example, many states passed tough laws to crack down on drunk drivers. A common practice was to hold first-time offenders who had not been in accidents in jail overnight to shame and frighten them into obeying the law.

Instead of reaching the desired outcome of a reduction in drunk drivers on the road, this policy resulted in a variety of outcomes. One was a jump in the number of people (mostly young men) who committed suicide in their cells while awaiting arraignment on drunk-driving charges. The self-imposed death penalty for a number of people for a traffic infraction is an example of how poorly experts design public policy about alcohol problems.

The vast majority arrested for drunk driving are troubled individuals with long-standing alcohol problems. Many others are people who, for one reason or another, consumed more alcohol than the law allows. Alcohol in high doses can exaggerate the mood of the moment. Locked up in a cell, humiliated and ashamed, these people with an underlying depression or other psychic pain find their circumstances unbearable enough for a jailhouse suicide.

Another area in which the experts are attempting to prevail is in the campaign to punish any driver who has used alcohol by reducing the blood alcohol concentration (BAC) from .10 percent to .08 percent or even .05 percent. The BAC can be used to define someone as legally drunk. The ultimate goal is to have any amount of alcohol in the blood viewed as a problem, even though all the accident data clearly show that the overwhelming majority of drunk driving accidents involve drivers with BACs well in excess of .10 percent.

The experts fail to see that broadening the definition of drunk driving will not help those who have problems with alcohol. Instead, it will reduce the likelihood that people with alcohol problems will find their way into treatment.

55

In addition, the measure of lowering the BAC, initiated during a time of recessionary cutbacks in local and state governments, would stretch available police and treatment resources to the breaking point.

The experts' obsession with alcohol as the cause of traffic accidents clouds the importance of other factors. Nearly four out of ten Americans believe that drunk driving is the most serious factor affecting highway safety, according to a recent Gallup survey. Yet improper driving, including speeding, making improper turns, failure to wear seat belts, and other operator errors, play a key role in 62 percent of all fatal automobile accidents and in 67 percent of all automobile accidents, according to the National Highway Traffic Safety Administration.

Sleep deprivation is another unmeasurable factor. According to some researchers in sleep behavior, sleep deprivation may be as responsible for automobile and other accidents as is alcohol.

During the early 1980s, public information efforts by anti-drunk driving groups endlessly repeated a staggering statistic: each year, over 25,000 people die in drunk driving accidents. The context for that figure, however, was always left out of the discussion. Additional data from the government's Fatal Accident Reporting System (FARS) reveals that 83 percent of these deaths can be considered self-imposed. Among those killed in drunk driving accidents, 52 percent are the drunk drivers themselves; another 20 percent are passengers who have chosen to ride with a drunk driver; and 11 percent are drunk pedestrians who walk in front of a car.

Certainly, even one innocent life lost is a tragedy. But the political effect of 4,250 innocent victims would be nowhere near as impressive as that of 25,000 innocent victims. In this instance, however, I don't think a conscious desire to mislead was the motivation for use of this incendiary statistic. Candy Lightner, the founder of Mothers Against Drunk Driving (MADD), had lost her teenage daughter in a drunk driving accident.

Many other activists who work for tougher drunk driving laws also have lost loved ones in senseless accidents. I am sure the magnitude of their losses could have made this statistic seem reasonable. Emotion is essential to experts and advocacy: the death of a beautiful young child killed by a drunk driver can inhibit objective examination of the issue.

In 1994, advocacy groups and government officials crowed that alcohol highway fatalities had fallen to 13,094. Eighty-nine percent, measured by the definitions noted above, were not innocent victims; 1,321 could be classified as innocent deaths, that is, people who were in the wrong place at the wrong time.

Guilt and Teen Drinking

Minimum Drinking Age Laced With Loopholes, Novello Says
                    —*Washington Post*, 12 September 1991

Novello Urges Tough Curbs on Liquor Ads, Says Industry 'Unabashedly' Targets Youth
                    —*Washington Post*, 5 November 1991

Two headlines from the *Washington Post* in late 1991 reinforce the belief that alcohol problems among teenagers are rampant. Again, the impression and the information from the experts are misleading. Teens are actually drinking less: according to a 1990 survey by the National Institute on Drug Abuse, 57 percent of high school seniors reported having had a drink in the past month, down from a peak of

72 percent in 1980. Among college freshman, the figure was 74.5 percent in 1990, down from 82 percent in 1980. In the obsession with finding foolproof legal methods to keep teens from drinking, hardly anyone notices the clear signs that educational messages, not fear and intimidation, are getting through to them.

Society's inability to see the value of education in preventing alcohol abuse is another feather in the cap of the experts who condemn alcohol. One of their most significant victories was the effort made to keep underage people from drinking by raising the drinking age to twenty-one. Many people actually opposed this effort by arguing that raising the drinking age to twenty-one was unwise when a young person's legal rights and responsibilities as a citizen begin at eighteen; but their protest was in vain.

Many groups chose to give in to the coercive and manipulative efforts of the experts. For example, state governments were told that they would receive additional funds to repair roadways only if they adopted twenty-one as their legal drinking age. This measure, although a victory for the experts, was a loss to those it purportedly protected. Some interpreted it as a message that drinking alcohol is somehow special, more adult even than driving, voting, serving on a jury, or going to war.

Using the statistical cudgel, the experts pointed to a decrease in the incidence of alcohol-related accidents for those under twenty-one after the drinking age was raised in the United States. What they neglected to point out was that the incidence of alcohol-related accidents for those under twenty-one fell by the identical amount in neighboring Canada, which did *not* raise its drinking age.

Prohibitions issued by adults simply serve to make alcohol an attractive forbidden fruit to young people. The minute we set something off limits, we rouse children's curiosity and their natural desire to test those limits. Consider the case of marijuana. In 1965, just 2 percent of people age sixteen to twenty-five had tried marijuana. By 1979, after fourteen years of society's attempts to control the drug's use by hammering home its dangers, 65 percent of young people had tried marijuana and 35 percent were regular users.

If the experts really wanted to stop drunk driving by teens, they would take an even more radical step and raise the driving age. Raising the driving age would prevent 65 percent of *all* teenage fatalities, including the ones in which alcohol use is a factor. But no one will ever seriously advance such a proposal.

By adopting the experts' narrow perspective on teen problems with alcohol, we may be missing the bigger picture. Consider one pertinent fact: despite the decline in teen drunk-driving deaths for several years, the overall teen death rate remained the same. In 1990, traffic crashes were the leading cause of death of Americans age sixteen to twenty; 3,361 young people died in alcohol-related traffic accidents in 1990.

Both the rate and number of these crashes have gone down in the past decade. At the same time, suicide among teens is the third-leading cause of death; the suicide rate among Americans age fifteen to nineteen has quadrupled in four decades from 2.7 per 100,000 in 1950 to 11.3 in 1988, and it continues to climb. Among people age fifteen to twenty-four, 5,000 kill themselves every year.

In addition to the youngsters who were successful in suicide, 1 in 12 high school students—or nearly 276,000 teenagers—tried to commit suicide in the past year, and more than 1 in 4 seriously contemplated it, according to a Centers for Disease Control study released in September 1990. Two percent—or 5,520—of the students who attempted to kill themselves suffered injuries severe enough to require medical attention.

The teen years are a perilous time. Perhaps the experts' focus on alcohol use among teens distracts them from seeing what could be the bigger picture of hopelessness and self-destructiveness that simply moves on from risk-taking behavior (such as drunk driving or binge drinking) to overtly suicidal behavior. Maybe society ought to ask itself why it is not listening to the painful outcries of teenagers.

Experts fall into a trap, and when we bow to their tyranny we follow them into their lair. In this case, the experts' single-minded focus on winning the battle against the evil of alcohol prevents them from seeing the entire picture. This blindness, and in turn other people's blindness, offers them a victory and strengthens their hold over our lives.

Rescinding Their Greatest Victory

We could strip the experts of their greatest victory by encouraging people to use alcohol responsibly in the same ways they encourage community action. For four thousand years, alcohol has been associated with treaties between nations, with religious rituals, and with the important events in an individual's life. Some recovered alcoholic people who otherwise abstain completely from alcohol take communal wine during religious services with no ill effects.

I feel that alcohol used in this way underscores the connections among us. It is part of what some of us share as members of the same church, the same social group, the same family, the same culture. Used properly, alcohol breaks down the barriers between people. They feel a little less alone, and the world seems a little less terrifying.

My experience is that alcohol's unique function is to release us to be present to each other in this changing reality. When alcohol is used in a social context with congeniality, not drunkenness, as the goal, it lifts most people out of the routine of ordinary living. In this way, alcohol differs from drugs such as marijuana, cocaine, and heroin, as well as from more solitary pursuits such as reading, watching television, and enjoying a fantasy life.

I have seen every ill and harm that alcohol can cause, and yet I still say that alcohol has done more good than harm, enhanced more lives than it has ruined. Those ruined lives are precious and for this reason I believe we have to do everything we can to promote humane and effective treatment for people who have problems with alcohol.

In order to begin breaking the hold of the experts, it is necessary to rescind their greatest victory. To do this, I believe we must adopt an attitude that accepts alcohol as a neutral substance whose effects are dose related, not as a wicked substance to be avoided or as a profoundly desirable substance to be sought. This attitude will do more to reduce alcohol problems than any expert's scheme to increase our guilt and shame.

Chapter 4

Malevolent Benefactors

A 29-year-old pregnant woman in Wyoming who was severely beaten by her husband went to a hospital for treatment. Among the tests the emergency room staff conducted was a test for alcohol in her system; when she tested positive, she was turned over to the police and charged with felony child abuse.

A small drama involving a battered wife and her unborn child encapsulates the ambiguities that occur when society, under the guidance of experts, uses simple, mechanical solutions to resolve complex social problems. In the hospital staff's hierarchy of victims, the abused wife ranked below the unborn fetus in requiring their protection. It was simpler to solve the problems of the unborn baby—administer a blood test, find traces of alcohol, charge the mother—than it was to deal with the problems of the mother—the complex circumstances of the woman's life. In this case, the charges against the woman were eventually dropped. But not everyone victimized by those who believe they are protectors of victims are so lucky.

Because of the large number of people labeled as victims, more people than ever fall under the protective and often misguided scrutiny of the social guardians—the law, the courts, the helping professions, the politicians, the special-

63

interest activists. These guardians intrude with an inflexible value system onto the fluid landscape of individual choice, with the goal of protecting someone's well-being.

People say, "I'm doing this for his own good. He doesn't know what's good for him, and I don't want to see him get hurt." That statement is fine if it is in the appropriate context, say that of a mother making a decision for her adolescent child; but it is not fine in most other contexts.

Unfortunately, this statement and its sentiment are repeatedly found in situations where one person or a group of people attempt to impose their beliefs and protection on others. In most cases, the protective actions wind up harming the very person targeted for protection. Instead of safeguarding the supposed victims, these actions protect the rest of us from knowing the true complexity of social problems and from dealing with root causes instead of tragic manifestations.

Manufacture of Victims

When tragedy strikes, being able to identify an "innocent victim" as someone who is subject to the whims of fate—dependent, unsuspecting, blameless—is a convenient label. A victim, therefore, presents no ambiguities and no confusing questions of responsibility to weigh and feel troubled about. The victim is innocent; therefore, someone or something else must be responsible.

When something bad happens to an innocent victim, especially one from those groups society views as vulnerable—children, women, and the elderly—our social guardians will feel justified in venting their most primitive emotions. I recall the pure anger of a store owner in New Hampshire, for example, when a four-year-old girl he didn't know was killed by a drunk driver. "Four years old," he kept saying, like a litany. He became angry with me when I asked whether it would have been different if the person killed had been an adult.

Victims also provide society with a simple way to think about complex social problems. When dealing with the problems of drugs, crime, poverty, traffic fatalities, and other social problems, our surrogate parents, the experts, seem to provide easy and fast solutions. Our social guardians focus their expertise on devising protective social policies for innocent victims, but neglect to deal with the underlying problems. They succeed in giving comfort in two ways.

First, their agenda allows other people to distance themselves from the plight of the victims. Second, by making the victim an emotional symbol, they can further their larger agenda: power and conformity. They define the situation as something that can be solved by simply finding and punishing the person or thing they view as responsible.

The manufacture of the label victim encourages a simplistic view of the world. It turns the world into good guys and bad guys, victims and victimizers, the innocent and the culpable. Life, however, is rarely that neat and simple. In seeing only black and white and ignoring the gray under the guise of protecting the innocent, great harm can be done.

Innocent Victims

The human fetus is the quintessential "innocent victim." Because the fetus is totally dependent on its mother for shelter, food, and safety, it qualifies for victim status and justifies strong protective measures. The idea that the fetus needs protection—even against the woman carrying it in her body—has been used by experts to justify a number of restrictions on pregnant women, such as taking alcohol, medicines, and so on.

Many of these restrictions, however, reflect our prejudices more than they address an authentic need. The specter of Fetal Alcohol Syndrome (FAS), for example, is a classic case of a small problem being blown out of proportion to achieve the hidden social end of prohibitionists. FAS is a complex distribution of birth defects appearing in a small number of babies born to some alcoholic mothers who drink heavy amounts of alcohol—ranging from ten to fourteen drinks a day. Contrary to popular belief, FAS is not a new phenomenon: centuries ago, physicians noted that some alcoholic women gave birth to "weak and feeble babies."

Never before our day has anyone suggested that *any* amount of alcohol could result in FAS. Yet within the past few years, the surgeon general of the United States issued an official statement warning women that they should completely avoid alcohol during pregnancy because "research had not established a safe level of alcohol intake."

The warning about FAS, from one of the top medical experts in the country, is right in line with our cultural prejudices about women's use of alcohol. Americans have always been uncomfortable about women's drinking. They are especially uncomfortable when a pregnant woman drinks.

Recently, a headline in the *New York Times* read "Use of Alcohol Linked to Rise in Fetal Illness." That is scary. But a careful reading of the article shows that, according to the Centers for Disease Control and Prevention (CDC), of the 9.4 million births that took place in the fourteen years between 1979 and 1993, 2,032 babies were born with health problems because their mothers drank alcohol during pregnancy.

In spite of this reality advocacy groups estimate that 4,000 to 8,000 babies are born each year with FAS—that is twenty-seven to fifty-five times higher than the actual numbers. They don't stop there. They go on to estimate that beyond the incidence of FAS, 55,000 other babies suffer unhealthy outcomes called fetal alcohol effects, and that the damage from drinking alcohol during pregnancy costs the country $1.6 billion a year.

Prejudices, however, should not form the basis of scientific warnings and legal policies like the one in Wyoming I cited at the beginning of this chapter. Common sense alone says that the surgeon general's warning is an overreaction. European countries with better infant mortality rates and infant health statistics than ours do not share America's hysteria over drinking during pregnancy. Women in Italy and France typically continue to drink moderately throughout pregnancy, but there is no evidence that these countries have as much of a problem about FAS as we do.

Recent studies reaffirm the finding that FAS is a danger only to women who are chronic excessive drinkers. In one of the largest studies ever conducted on FAS, scientists reviewed the pregnancy outcomes and drinking habits of 12,000 women. Of these, 204 were identified by their own report as abusive drinkers (ten to fourteen drinks a day). Five FAS babies were born to women in the study, all of them to mothers who drank abusively.

The general overreaction about FAS has gone even further in the case of women who are addicted to drugs like cocaine or crack. In places around the country, these women are being charged with the crime of "fetal abuse" and are being separated from their children, prosecuted, and jailed.

In 1990, for example, twenty-three-year-old Jennifer Johnson of Florida, a crack addict, was convicted of distributing drugs to a minor through the umbilical cord. Because a fetus has no legal standing under Florida law, the district attorney carefully drew up the charge, limiting it to the moments after the baby was born but before the umbilical cord was cut. If Johnson had not smoked crack a few hours before going into labor, the case would never have gone to trial. The court found Johnson guilty and sentenced her to fifteen years' probation, contingent on her entering a drug-treatment center and getting a job.

The irony of the case is that Johnson sought treatment when she found out she was pregnant. The drug-treatment programs in her county, however, had a waiting list of over two thousand. In addition, Johnson had no job skills and was repeatedly turned down on job interviews. In the law's hierarchy of victims, there was no way to see Johnson herself as a victim of the very system that was prosecuting her. Because it's believed that "good" women will do anything for their babies, Johnson becomes a "bad" woman needing to be punished for having a drug problem.

Fetal abuse prosecution is a case of expert technology outstripping social consensus on use. Cases like Johnson's are revealed by a blood test for newborns that can tell if drugs are in the mother's system near the time of birth. Babies born in public hospitals are routinely tested if their mothers are young, unmarried, poor, Black, or Hispanic.

The test, however, is not foolproof. Recently, a woman who tested positive for drugs challenged the result when she was forcibly separated from her newborn child. The drugs detected were not taken recreationally by the mother, but were medically administered during labor.

Courts across the United States use the results of these tests to prosecute women, especially poor women, in the name of protecting a victim, the unborn baby. Yet, at the same time, the United States ranks nineteenth in the world in infant mortality and twenty-first in mortality of children under five. Costa Rica, Jamaica, and Sri Lanka have infant mortality rates lower than Washington, D.C. However, the experts spend time and money on prosecuting mothers for fetal abuse instead of improving prenatal care, which has been repeatedly shown to be the one factor that improves pregnancy outcomes.

By focusing on use of substances as the litmus test for the proper care of a fetus, the experts and society avoid measures to reduce the greatest threat to fetuses and babies: maternal poverty. Bigger and healthier babies typically are born to middle-class women who have good incomes and are properly fed and housed, even if the mother is young, uneducated, or unmarried.

The FAS babies are far more likely to be born to Black alcoholic mothers than to White alcoholic mothers, a reflection of the White mothers' generally higher socioeconomic status. The threat of fetal abuse prosecution may keep poor women away from the social services and health services where prenatal care is available.

Catch-22 of Protection

Protection is a solution spouted fervently by experts as an action-oriented, "do-something" approach to problem solving. Do-something approaches to social problems rarely do any good. They make the doers feel superior and self-important because they have done *something*. In many cases, do-something approaches actually harm the victims.

For example, anyone who has spent time working in education and prevention knows that ubiquitous warnings and threats of prosecution do not reach the people to whom they are directed: alcoholic women, women addicted to drugs, and women involved in other self-endangering behaviors. These women are acting under a compulsion: they are medicating pain and coping with a harsh environment. Nothing will help them except a change in their basic life circumstances.

Instead, the wholesale warnings about FAS by experts, in this case, by one of the top medical experts in the United States, chiefly frighten the women who are most likely to listen to warnings but who are least in danger of having children with FAS. Many of these women become obsessively concerned about their alcohol intake. One researcher noted that some women became concerned if they inadvertently took even an insignificant amount of alcohol, as in wine vinegar. This unnecessary stress, they suggested, may itself be harmful to mother and fetus.

Similar catch-22 situations abound where experts rush in to protect the fetus and newborn from mothers who are considered unfit. In many cases, for example, children are taken away from these mothers who love and cherish them, but who live in situations where they are unable to help themselves care properly for their children. In return for this protection from their mothers, these children often find themselves lost in a foster care system that in many cases does more harm than good.

Furthermore, when experts label children as "crack babies" or "FAS infants" they disregard the possibility that this stigmatization may make the children victims of their protectors, not of the drug. Because it is difficult to find foster homes or adoptive families for children with such problems, many crack and FAS babies born to poor women spend months or even years as "boarder babies" in hospitals.

Experts make assumptions about the behavior of these children based on limited knowledge and insight. They do not know how much of these children's withdrawn states, slow developments, and behavioral problems comes because they are deprived of love and stability.

Protecting Women

Women have always been considered victims of their biology. Because of their special role as bearers of children, they have been considered delicate, fragile, weak, and emotional. These characteristics, in turn, have been used by many societal experts as reasons for keeping women out of jobs, public office, and other spheres that require strength, toughness, and emotional stability.

When women began to win social equality in the 1970s and 1980s, the first stereotypes to go were the biologically linked ones. However, the medical, biological, and legal experts are reclaiming women as victims of their biology.

Women are rightfully suspicious of advice that sounds like old restrictions in new guises. As I mentioned in chapter 2, millions of women consider themselves victims of premenstrual syndrome (PMS). PMS is a new name for the old belief that women were emotionally unstable during menstruation.

The protection, in many cases, places women into another set of catch-22s. For example, women's groups and the female members of Congress have been saying that the National Institutes of Health (NIH) has not funded enough studies using women as subjects. The NIH responded to the inequity by publishing guidelines for women as study subjects. The guidelines precluded administering a variety of drugs to women that might affect a

71

developing fetus, on the chance they might be or become pregnant. Since most drugs used in clinical studies have unknown effects on pregnancy, the guidelines, set up to protect women and their unborn children, effectively barred all women of childbearing age from inclusion in important health studies.

American society has always frowned on women going to war. During the Persian Gulf war, the sight of women in the active military, and especially the military reserve, tearfully saying goodbye to their children upset many people. For a while, Congress considered a number of bills that would have prevented mothers (or fathers who had sole custody of their children) from being called up to go to war.

The problem, however, was that many of these women had joined the military because they were supporting their children. If they were blocked from doing jobs that might be needed in time of war, they would be barred from the higher-paying military jobs that also carry opportunities for advancement. The decision makers won't ever have to see the sad spectacle of those tearful goodbyes again. And what they don't see—women trying to make ends meet in low-paying jobs with impossible hours—doesn't worry them.

If people really wanted to protect women and their children, they would devote more social and creative energy and money to real solutions, not sham protection. In Germany, for example, every family receives a monthly cash payment during a child's first six months of life and additional payments until the child is sixteen.

The German tax exemption for each dependent is more than twice the one given to Americans. Child care costs parents one-seventh of what it does in the United States. German parents automatically receive free health-care coverage for their dependents on their personal health-care insurance policy. A German high school teacher is on the same pay scale as a government lawyer or physician. German universities are free. A German family receives a special tax deduction of $1,000 per year per child for eight years to build or buy a home. These are just the general benefits. Special additional payments go to poor families.

In the United States, formal social support for families above the poverty level is a $2,000 personal exemption for dependents and tax-subsidized public schools. Until recently, teachers were among the lowest-paid professionals. Day-care workers still are underpaid.

Public policy to encourage better parenting in our society is given a low priority by the experts, especially in recessionary times. Instead of offering real solutions for the problems people face in their day-to-day family lives, experts give empty rhetoric about family values and spending more "quality time" together. But who addresses the problem of how these people are supposed to find the money to feed and shelter their children?

A survey recently showed that parents spent thirty hours a week with their children in 1965 and only seventeen hours a week in 1985. Children's Market Research of New York says today's kids spend an average of three hours a day with their parents. Most of the difference is taken up by parents having to work more to care for their families.

Romance of Childhood

Like the New Hampshire store owner I mentioned earlier, most of us become very emotional when we think harm is being done to children. This rush of emotion is a way of venting some of our own deep ambivalence. Most parents are so hopelessly guilt-ridden about what they do and don't do for their children that they let experts, who they clearly believe know best, stir them up about imaginary risks.

No one wants to acknowledge the brutal truths of our society. For example, in the United States almost all problems of children are associated with the quality of the strength and stability of the family. Like the man I met on the airplane who feared child kidnappers but didn't know that most of them were noncustodial parents, we are far more comfortable looking for child victimizers and other culpable people "out there" than facing the fact that society just doesn't care.

In the mid-1980s, in schools across the country, the old adage "never talk to strangers" took on a new meaning. Following the example of the public service announcements by McGruff, television's crime watchdog whose job was to "take a bite out of crime," local police departments developed a program on "strangers" for elementary schools.

The children were taught that simply not talking to or taking rides from people they did not know was not enough. It was necessary to identify the threat of a stranger by continually repeating the word "stranger." Children as young as four and five could be heard chanting, "stranger, stranger, stranger" whenever a person they did not know stopped to talk to them. To my knowledge, the children were never warned of possible harm by those people they knew.

Even some of our most persistent urban legends of stranger-danger are ultimately proof that children are more at risk at home than from the outside world. Every year, parents become panicky about the so-called Halloween sadists who poison or booby-trap candy handed out to children. Yet when two researchers examined seventy-six specific incidents between 1958 and 1984, they found that no deaths or serious injuries were linked to treats given by strangers.

In several of the incidents, children booby-trapped the candy themselves. In two highly publicized cases in which the children died, the father of one child and an uncle of the other were the actual perpetrators. This frantic and constant fear of outside danger helps distract people from the really frightening facts of children's lives.

Children are human beings at their best. The energy, curiosity, openness, and honesty of young children is sheer delight. But they require a safe haven to return to when something in the outside world sets them back. And society could readily provide such systems of support and comfort today. But impugning the motives of strangers has won out over progressive thinking.

This form of child neglect manifests itself most strikingly when that lovable child passes into the difficult teenage years, and becomes a challenge. Teens vacillate between being the dependent child and the independent grown-up. The teens are, by any definition, a tough time. Teen suicides, the third-leading cause of death among fifteen to twenty-four-year olds, are double what they were twenty years ago. Our discomfort about discussing suicidal feelings with teens may contribute to the problem. One of my colleagues, a bright and able hospital administrator, discussed his teenager's depression with me. He reported that when his son told him how depressed he felt about his life this bright and able man said, "How can you feel so down? These are the best years of your life."

The father's response may have encouraged inadvertently the child's suicidal fantasies. If the boy felt that these were the best years of his life and he felt so horrible, it is easy to see how suicide could look like a reasonable escape from his suffering. Society is highly susceptible to the romanticized relationship of parent and child created by the experts. Ofttimes this image of a parent-child relationship blurs our vision, and we miss the opportunity to intervene when the child is truly in danger.

Despite the abundance of expert advice, our teen pregnancy rate is higher than that of other industrialized nations, even when compared to countries in which the rates of teen sexual activity are comparable. Each year, one out of ten teenage girls becomes pregnant. The rate of teenage pregnancies is much higher because the prevailing wisdoms believe ignorance leads to abstinence. Most of us are locked into a "Just Say No" simplicity.

The same thinking is at work in the debate over whether the schools should teach teenagers about condoms to prevent pregnancy and protect against AIDS. The issue is often talked about in abstract terms: parental rights, the limits of school interference, where values are learned, and other lofty concepts. The subject, however, is a question of life and death. Parents and experts who live by the rule that ignorance leads to abstinence refuse to admit they are willing implicitly to condemn to death (psychologically, in the case of teen pregnancy, or literally, in the case of AIDS) children who follow their hormones instead of their parents' dictates. The best theory of abstinence I know of for young and old alike is the thesis of self-respect: being able to resist temptation because it does not fit into a person's self-image.

Underestimating the Protected

Many parents and concerned adults earnestly believe that in protecting children, they should avoid real conversation on subjects such as sex and suicide. In this case, they choose to either underestimate the child's intellectual and spiritual capacities or underrate their own ability to discuss the subject in a sensitive and helpful manner. A similar parallel is seen in the spirit of protection by those who think that the poor and undereducated and now people without degrees or credentials are not sufficiently knowledgeable to make wise decisions about their lives.

A number of advocacy groups too numerous to list, for example, have been trying to prevent targeted advertising on alcohol, tobacco, tennis shoes, fast food, and a host of other products to Blacks, Hispanics, women, teenagers, and children. The point of their protest is that corporations profit at the expense of groups that can be easily seduced (or can't resist the urge) to go the happy, destructive route portrayed and promoted.

The belief that advertising has enormous power over the young and the poor shows a remarkable disrespect for them. An advocacy group cited with alarm the fact that the average child sees 100,000 beer commercials before age twenty-one. If alcohol advertising is so powerful, why does a third of the American public grow up to be nondrinkers? Research outcome proves that young people are not like machines, nor are they like Pavlov's dogs. They make their important decisions based on more than pictures and jingles.

Blacks, Hispanics, women, and children grow up and live reasonable lives in spite of the intentions of those who are out to protect them. Nothing I know of convinces me that white males are either more or less susceptible to advertising and promotion than any other group. The only ones who profit from these efforts are the advocacy groups, not the people they contend they are trying to help.

Stigmas and Self-Fulfilling Prophesies

Much of the time, the help given to people who are supposed to need protection only manages to stigmatize them. A number of prominent Blacks, for example, have begun to grapple with the fact that being hired for any job, even a prestigious one, under an affirmative action program creates a stigma. Many children are stigmatized as "learning disabled." A recent study showed that two-thirds or more of first-grade children who had been diagnosed with dyslexia by the fifth grade no longer show signs of it. Parents accept the stigma because having a labeled child is better than having a stupid child. The child gets an identity and a comforting reason for failure. Schools do not have to deal with the real problems of poorly trained teachers and inadequately funded programs.

The disabled are easily stigmatized by well-meaning help. A blind activist for the disabled said that the most crippling handicap for her was being seen as one of "Jerry's kids." Telethons, she said, romanticize the plucky, indomitable spirit of some people with disabilities while subtly implying that those who don't surmount obstacles are bad or lazy or inferior. By "telethonizing" the disabled, she said, society was able to emotionally justify doing nothing to reduce the physical barriers that keep the disabled from leading more normal lives.

Like all protection, the protection offered to those who accept a social stigma is a catch-22. While it may temporarily ease the pain of difference, ultimately it guarantees that the stigmatized will have their lives defined by others, not by their own efforts. Like all protection, the innocent victim, who may or may not have started out as a real victim, becomes an iatrogenic victim—victimized by the supposed cure for his or her disease.

Protection Begins Within

However well-meaning the experts in their roles as social guardians and protectors, their protection will always be an illusion. People typically solve their own problems when they are supposedly trying to solve the problems of others. If some social phenomenons such as crack babies or soldier-mothers pains them, they try to ease their own pain in the guise of helping the victim.

Many victims don't want the protection offered to them. They resent the implication of the idea that somehow they have been disenfranchised. When the experts and those of us who follow the experts tell us what's good for victims, we do not hear what the victims want to state for themselves. The belief exists that whatever victims say and do when speaking out on their own behalf will not be what we have deemed as the "right" thing for them.

Real protection starts from within. Nearly everyone can make reasonable and intelligent choices if they are given real choices. Jennifer Johnson tried to "protect" herself and her child, but could find neither a bed in a treatment program nor a job. If the experts would not try to solve complex problems with simple solutions, Jennifer Johnson and millions like her might have a fighting chance. We must always remember that we are all born with a powerful life force: the instinct for self-preservation.

Chapter 5

Partisans of Utopia

Biosphere 2, the mini-earth constructed under a glass dome in the Arizona desert, is foundering in waste gases. Despite years of planning, $150 million in private investments and the involvement of scores of reputable scientists, no one has been able to figure out how to make the atmosphere self-sustaining. Hours before the dome was sealed for a two-year experiment in self-contained living, a carbon-dioxide scrubber was secretly brought in to keep the air from becoming unbreathable.

—Joel Achenbach

More disappointing than the problems with Biosphere 2 were the expectations everyone had for it. Few people ever seemed to doubt that scientists could build a working model of the earth on three acres. Even now, few of the project's critics question the premise of the venture. Instead, the scientists involved are rushing to accuse Space Biosphere Ventures, the private company that conceived and financed the project, of cutting corners and making the experiment scientifically invalid. Space Biosphere Ventures, for its part, refuses to admit the carbon dioxide scrubber compromises its original plan.

Biosphere 2 is a cautionary parable for the environmental movement, the most powerful political advocacy movement

81

of the 1990s. After two decades, environmentalism has a cachet that other movements would give their eyeteeth for. Chemical manufacturers make environmental claims in their television advertising. Products from detergents to trash bags declare themselves environmentally friendly. In the movies, the good guys are those characters with an environmental conscience. In *The Prince of Tides*, for example, a psychiatrist asks the hero what is troubling him. "The greenhouse effect," he responds. "Acid rain."

Environmental experts, like consumer groups and ad hoc groups advocating specific public policies, build a constituency by identifying problems and then promising to tell us how to protect ourselves. They touch our vulnerabilities, and we readily align ourselves with their positions. People are more willing to follow the advice of environmental groups than the Environmental Protection Agency (EPA).

Yet Biosphere 2 demonstrates on a small scale how specious the advocates' pretensions to knowledge are and how far from reality they may be. It also demonstrates how vulnerable we are to the comforting sense of control that advocates offer over a mysterious and complex world. We believe that even though we may not know what global warming is nor understand its effects, there are others out there who do, and they are looking out for our best interests.

Experts, as we have seen, pervade all areas of our lives. They confront and often prey upon our doubts and fears by telling us what to do, what to think, and what is good for us. Essentially, they tell us how to live. It is not enough for them to disseminate information, they also make the choices for us. They make predictions and offer solutions based on limited and often flawed information. Their grasp reaches even beyond our everyday lives.

Natural Life Cycle of Advocacy

The environmental movement is a textbook example of the natural life cycle of political advocacy groups. Such groups start out with well-meaning people who have an important message and a mission to capture the public's attention. Once they have our attention, however, they're caught in a trap. If they solve the problem, they're out of a job; but if they don't solve it, they'll lose the public's attention.

So the next step, without realizing the consequences, is to broaden the definition of the problem. The logic seems reasonable: Nothing exists in a vacuum, thus the problem must affect other situations. This leads to a pattern of upping the ante as the problem grows more intractable and more immediate than first considered. This process is much like addiction in which larger doses of the addictive substance are needed to get the same effect.

In the late 1960s and early 1970s, the environmental movement entered the first stage of its life cycle. A strange mix of conservationists and sportspeople composed its main constituency. As accounts of environmental problems were publicized, awareness and concern spread across the country. Part of this was the "Give a hoot, don't pollute" campaign of Woodsy the Owl and friends. Along with sudden awareness of the country's polluted air, water, and soil came the environmental experts' finger-pointing predictions of impending doom.

Concrete evidence of short-sighted environmental solutions of the past was everywhere. Lakes and rivers were closed to fishing and swimming because of pollution. The air in major cities was thick with smog. Industrial chemicals could literally crop up in someone's backyard, as in Love Canal, New York. Within a few years the environmentalists

83

had achieved many of their aims. Laws and regulations were enacted to govern the long, slow process of cleaning up the country's environment. Despite the imperfections of the political system, progress came quickly.

The environmentalists, predictably, did not go out of business. Instead, they went global. The major environmental groups shifted their focus to new problems: acid rain, global warming, the ozone layer, old-growth forests, and extinction of species. Although these issues are far less clearly understood by the scientific community than are water and air pollution, the environmentalists have imparted their credibility to their presentation of them.

Return to the Garden

The connecting link between the environmentalists' local and global focus is the belief that the "natural" or undeveloped state of the earth is the ideal state. Nearly all the industrial developments of the past two centuries—manufacturing, electrical generation, petrochemicals, nuclear power—have been fingered as the cause of environmental problems.

Right or wrong, these warnings strike a deep emotional chord in many Americans. Always given to romanticizing the American frontier and life on the land, Americans fell in love with ideas like "sustainable societies," "small is beautiful," solar power, and organic gardening. Easily made to feel guilty about our American standard of living, we eagerly adopted the creed that there would be plenty of everything to go around if we used a little less and recycled a little more. Some baby boomers, who disdained consumerism in the 1960s, chose symbolic gestures such as using cloth diapers to assuage their guilt.

Environmentalism reveals a characteristically American

contradiction: although we live in the most technologically advanced civilization on earth, a deep and unreasoning fear of technology haunts many of us. Except in the case of our automobiles, which environmentalists have said for decades are a wasteful luxury, many of us are inclined to believe any evil the environmental experts tell us about technology.

The less control we have over our exposure to high technology, the more we harbor the secret fear that it could harm us. Even ordinary 60-Hertz electric currents—perhaps the most ubiquitous of all our environmental alterations—have been implicated in causing mental disorders and childhood leukemia. Although the accusation clearly does not square with the fact that life expectancies have doubled since the beginning of industrialization, the suspicions persist.

At the same time, we have a naive belief that anything "natural"—not manufactured—is safe and benign. In a recent Roper poll, manufactured chemicals were ranked at the top of a list of public concerns. Cancer researchers, however, estimate that such chemicals cause less than a fraction of 1 percent of cancer deaths, while radon, a naturally produced gas, is believed responsible for 2 to 3 percent of cancer deaths.

Natural carcinogens, in fact, are ten times more likely to cause cancer than are manufactured carcinogens. The natural rays of the sun account for 30 percent of all cancers. At the same time, some chemical preservatives used in food processing are believed to help protect against cancer of the stomach. Nowhere is it written that nature and its natural wonders are benign.

Apocalyptic Fears

Besides these powerful appeals to emotions, environmentalists and other advocates appeal to the human desire for order. In the past, this need for order was filled by a belief in absolutes. During the Middle Ages, for example, nearly everyone believed God would cause the downfall of rulers who misused their dominion over a land, its people, and its goods. Implied in this belief was a divinely ordained and universally acknowledged standard for "right use" of the earth. The teachings of the church and the code of knighthood incorporated the standard and led to waging "just wars" to defend the misuse of the land.

All advocates, but particularly environmentalists, are the inheritors of these medieval beliefs. Advocates view the political process as a grand struggle between right and wrong, with the balance always on the verge of tipping irrevocably to the wrong. A collection of direct-mail letters from advocacy groups to constituents would make an interesting contribution to a sealed one-hundred-year time capsule. The people of the 2090s would wonder how the earth had survived such dangerous times.

Environmentalists, because they deal with the fate of the earth, conjure up grand apocalyptic visions. Imagery of destruction suffuses environmental rhetoric: acid rain will kill lakes and depopulate forests; global warming will stir up the seas, disrupt growing seasons, and make whole continents uninhabitable. This apocalypse is upon us, they warn. Because the government and corporations have the power to misuse the environment, their failure to protect us heralds impending doom.

More Questions than Answers

If the environmentalists' predictions and fears are correct, and our planet is indeed on the brink of destruction, the environmentalists would be prophets. But despite their emotional appeals and their apocalyptic vision, the environmentalists' view—like any advocate's view—is distinctly one-sided.

In spite of this gloomy picture, the chief environmental issues of our day are far from understood. Consider, for example, two popular issues worrying us today: global warming and acid rain. As for global warming, all scientists agree that some global warming is taking place, but no one actually knows how much. Scientists have kept worldwide temperature records only since the late 1800s—not nearly enough time to measure trends on a four and a half billion-year-old planet.

Environmental scientists make their predictions about global warming on computer simulations. But these are based only on the data available, and many scientists admit that makes them too ill-equipped to predict anything.

Some scientists even suggest that other ecological disturbances will cancel the effects of global warming. For example, sulfur dioxide—the chemical largely responsible for acid rain—might seed clouds in the atmosphere and so cool the planet, maintaining a rough equilibrium over time.

Recent studies seem to indicate that the experts and the advocates may have overreacted. The following quote, taken from a story by columnist William Raspberry in the *Washington Post*, sheds new light on global warming and the depletion of the ozone layer.

Attempts to detect the most feared effect of ozone depletion—increased bombardment of the Earth's surface by UV rays—have failed to turn up any evidence of increased ultraviolet influx outside the Antarctic region during the few weeks each year that the ozone hole is open.

If there has been any increase in UV, researchers say, it is too small to measure against a background of normal ultraviolet levels that

87

rise and fall by large amounts for entirely natural reasons on time scales from hours to decades.

Like global warming, the issues involved in acid rain are far from understood. The environmentalists believe acid rain is destroying forests and lakes, and they can produce many studies on the short-term effects to support their point. But a project undertaken by the federal government, the National Acid Precipitation Assessment Program, came to a different conclusion.

The study, although singular in nature, was conducted over a period of ten years to assess the long-term effects of acid rain and found "no evidence of a general or unusual decline of forests in the U.S. and Canada due to acid rain," except in red spruce at high altitudes. The acid damage to about 10 percent of eastern lakes, the study found, had gotten no worse since 1980. The study did find that acid rain contributes to erosion of buildings and statues. The government spent many years and much money on the study, but environmentalists have generally dismissed it, and it has gone largely unreported in the press.

Doomsday Averted

Environmentalists, as prophets, have a poor track record. As with the Biosphere 2 experiment, nature repeatedly shows us how little we know about how the world works.

After the ship *Exxon Valdez* hit the rocks of Prince William Sound in 1989, for example, environmentalists predicted a virtual end to Alaska's salmon industry. Yet in the 1990 fishing season, the Alaskan fleet caught more than 40 million salmon, surpassing the 1987 record catch of 29 million. In 1991, Alaskan pink salmon were so abundant that they far exceeded the demand by processors. Fishermen had to get rid of more than 10 million netted fish, dumping some and sending the rest to the Soviet Union as part of a humanitarian airlift.

A particularly embarrassing example of how difficult it is to outguess nature is the story of the snail darter, the three-inch minnow that brought the endangered-species issue to the public's attention. In 1978, the Supreme Court blocked the completion of the Tellico Dam in Tennessee because the dam would threaten the habitat of the only known population of the fish. Congress later overrode the decision by legislation to complete the dam, and environmentalists everywhere lamented the loss of yet another species to progress.

Yet the snail darter did not die. In August 1983, the U.S. Fish and Wildlife Service removed the snail darter from the federal endangered species list. To their surprise, they had found many populations of snail darters throughout the Tennessee River Valley.

Environmentalists are not alone in underestimating the self-regulating power of the natural and political worlds. The nuclear disarmament movement, for example, predicted nuclear disaster, not to mention economic ruin, if the United States did not unilaterally disarm. It did not foresee that economic and social forces in the Soviet Union would accomplish in a year what their movement could not in four decades.

The failure of the experts, environmental or others, to predict future conditions is inevitable. It is not possible because they are up against too many negative factors. First, experts suffer from a narrow focus and an inability to see beyond their own noses. When they make predictions, they do not allow for chance or fate, because it is impossible to control for all factors.

89

Second, the power to answer questions, address concerns of the masses, and dictate the directions of people's lives—God's role—is a seductive aphrodisiac that often blurs reality. The experts get so ensnared in the importance and grandeur of their own ideals and powers that they can no longer put the problem or the solution into perspective.

When Institutions Fail

If environmentalists are wrong so often, how is it that they so thoroughly control the debate over the planet's future? I believe their success is a sign of the failure of government and other institutions to provide credible alternatives.

Government, for example, all too often appears to be enmeshed in conflicts of interest, too involved with the industries it regulates to be impartial. Many of the people who prepare or enforce environmental regulations, for example, either come from or go to jobs in the industries they regulate. The laws on environmental issues, too, often seem fraught with loopholes and are too lumbering to enforce.

Science, too, does not seem to merit trust. In his book *News and Numbers,* journalist Victor Cohn quotes Tim Hammonds of the Food Marketing Institute: "Many have come to feel that for every Ph.D., there is an equal and opposite Ph.D." Scientific disciplines do not see their ultimate responsibility as producing something of human use, so they have no mechanism for building scientific consensus or communicating that consensus.

Some people become frustrated when science cannot give a straight answer about simple issues, such as whether to put babies in cloth or disposable diapers. A study sponsored by Proctor and Gamble found that cloth diapers are more costly to the environment than disposables; a study for the National Association of Diaper Services found just the opposite.

Public confidence in scientific institutions is at an all-time low. We want someone to believe in, someone without a vested interest, whose claims of corruption corroborate our experience of having been conned. The prevailing belief holds that there are answers somewhere, and that the advocates must have them, since no one else seems to.

Advocacy as Institution

Merely because people want unequivocal answers, however, does not mean they exist. Although environmentalists and other advocates portray themselves as outsiders of the system, working against the entrenched power of institutions, advocacy itself is an institution. In the past two decades, the number of advocacy groups in operation has grown by 328 percent. In 1970, there were 828 advocacy groups operating in the health and science area; by 1990, there were 2,162. In public affairs, the number of advocacy groups rose from 532 in 1970 to 2,292 in 1990.

As an institution, advocacy is subject to the same criticisms as the institutions it attacks. For example, although advocates like to point the finger at corporate greed, advocates also have financial motives. They need money to keep their organizations afloat and to publicize their causes. The Natural Resources Defense Council (NRDC), for example, was sued for a 1989 publicity campaign devised by a media consultant who was hired by the group to help expand its membership base.

Acting on the consultant's advice, NRDC released a

91

report estimating that the growth-regulating chemical Alar, used chiefly on apples, might cause as many as 5,300 childhood cancers. After widespread media attention, the manufacturer withdrew the chemical from the market, and supermarkets posted signs assuring their customers they would never sell Alar-treated apples again.

Not long afterwards, it became clear that the dangers from Alar were grossly exaggerated. The California Department of Food and Agriculture studied the NRDC report and other studies, then calculated the probable risks of Alar at three and a half more cases of cancer for every one trillion apple eaters. The NRDC apologized; the suit was dismissed, but the apple growers sustained losses of $100 million.

More often than money, the need to be a player in the vast game of special-interest politics motivates an advocate as strongly as it does a politician or a bureaucrat. As in other institutions, the drive for power can be ruthless, pitting the advocate's ostensible motivations against the needs of the "cause."

The Issue of Smoking

I think the smoking-health issue illustrates how the experts operate. First, the antismoking advocates attack the advertising of tobacco products. They firmly state (without credible evidence) that advertisements make people take up smoking. In the mind of the antismoking advocates, people are like dogs who respond mindlessly to suggestion. It does not take much thinking to see how such a conclusion—that people are being manipulated into unhealthy behavior—would rile the public. In the case of children, many people feel guilty enough to start with. The public health advocates, with the help of some children who are artful at manipulation, make it sound like the hungry-for-the-dollar (standard practice in free enterprise) businesspeople hook children and others on smoking.

Since children and adults are individuals possessing some freedom of choice, the phenomenon of addiction is brought in. There has never been a question in my mind that a person can become addicted to anything, but I have yet to meet an addicting substance. An addicting substance means that anyone who uses it cannot go without it. I know of no such substance.

Let me tell about my own smoking history. I was a pipe smoker while in college and medical school because it was fashionable to smoke a pipe. And as a psychiatrist, smoking a pipe helped me to control my tendency to talk too much. I used my pipe to keep my mouth shut, so I could listen to my patients.

When I became a mover and shaker in government, pipe smoking was impossible. I had to move quickly and often. Meetings, gatherings, and all the hullabaloo that comes with power did not permit the leisure a pipe requires. So I turned to cigarettes and smoked three packs a day.

As I approached the end of my tenure at NIAAA, one of my sons bet me twenty dollars that I could not go one year without smoking. From the day I left office, I did not smoke for one year, collected the twenty bucks he owed me, and went back to cigarette smoking, but not to three packs a day.

People who were smokers and could not quit told me I must not have been addicted. In other words, if the facts don't fit a preconceived model, you don't throw out the model; you disregard the facts that threaten the model.

It appears to me, therefore, that the antismoking advocates think that at first children are hooked by advertising

93

and then when they grow up and become sensible adults, they can't give up the habit because they are physiologically addicted. One question that the antismoking advocates have never sought to answer is: does the emphasis on cigarettes being addictive prevent people who would want to from stopping?

I have seen this kind of propaganda in alcoholism treatment as well. People who are recovering from alcohol problems are told their only hope for recovery is total abstinence; if they slip, they'll fail. When they do fail it's because they have been indoctrinated to expect to fail. This corroborates my contention that expectation is as strong a drug as most substances.

Whenever people worry about the effects advertising has on children, I am reminded of the letter a young person wrote to the *New York Times*, "We make our choices even though we know the risks." It's good to remember what Winston Churchill said: "When I get the facts, I twist them to fit my position." Churchill was telling us what the experts do, but he was disarmingly honest about it. Having said that, let us look at what's happening in the tobacco industry.

Public health advocates claim the industry tricks young people to smoke through targeted marketing, advertising, and promotion, and once manipulated (especially when they are not of an age to know better) into smoking, they are physiologically hooked. But methods of manipulation can be artfully unfair, insidious, and omnivorous. Consider the phenomenon called environmental tobacco smoke (ETS).

Studies are legion that link the health risks of second-hand smoke to cancer, sudden infant death syndrome (SIDS), heart disease, and every other ailment imaginable.

These studies are flawed because they cannot be controlled, yet they epitomize how science is used to manipulate the public and policy makers. There is no scientific methodology available I know of that will give us the data to determine if a smoker does harm to a nonsmoker. Of course, scientists can come up with statistical models that will provide numbers that will imply certainty where certainty cannot exist.

The *Washington Times* on 27 November 1995 reported on a new service that accuses government and antismoking groups of making unsubstantiated claims about the health hazards of second-hand smoke. The Congressional Research Service claims there is no scientific evidence to support the EPA estimate that environmental tobacco smoke (ETS) causes over 3,000 lung-cancer deaths among nonsmokers and 150,000 to 300,000 cases of respiratory infection in infants and young children.

Like the antialcohol advocates whose exaggerated findings on FAS led the government to advise pregnant women not to drink alcohol, nonsmoking advocates continue to use unsubstantiated studies to induce the public and policy makers to treat smokers as pariahs.

Crucial to the accuracy of scientific study is controlling for variables. For example, if a person smokes X number of cigarettes around a nonsmoker, the variables to control for would be the setting, the ventilation system, air streams, depth of inhalation and exhalation of both parties, emotional strengths and weaknesses (which affect the immunological system), and hundreds of other variables. Even so the advocates use the flawed studies on ETS to promote their cause, gain power, and feel good about themselves. No better illustration exists than cigarettes to show the tyranny of the experts.

95

Chapter Five

Radical Activists

Among some radical groups, the drive for power edges over the border into fanaticism. Radical environmentalists in the Northwest, for example, damage machinery belonging to logging companies and endanger loggers in the process. They also drive metal stakes into trees to make them unfit for logging. If a staked tree is inadvertently sent to the sawmill, it could cause a serious accident.

These radical activists are fanatics: they must save the old-growth forests at any cost, regardless of what anyone else wants or what the majority dictates. Like many fanatics, they defend their actions with a dangerous thesis: the end justifies the means. Unfortunately, society has been seduced by this thesis, which harbors the false impression that noise and radical behavior make a committed and righteous expert.

Advocates are largely silent about the moral ambiguities of such behavior, but they are rarely reticent about questioning the motives of others. To accomplish this, their typical and most successful line of attack is by implication. For example, when I took unpopular stands as director of the National Institute on Alcohol Abuse and Alcoholism (NIAAA), activists would imply that I was in the pay of the alcohol-beverage industry. It made no difference that in my long career in the field I tangentially received only two small grants from the industry. One, for $2,500, was awarded to Massachusetts General Hospital where I worked to study new ways of motivating alcoholic people to seek treatment. The other was an unsolicited payment of $700, half of which was retained by my publisher, to reprint a part of my first popular book on alcohol.

Those who question a researcher's funding need prove no direct influence. The damage is in the inference. A

96

funding source can affect a study's credibility with the public. Elizabeth Whelan, Ph.D., whose American Council on Science and Health is frequently attacked by environmentalists and consumer advocates because it receives some funding from the chemical industry, wrote that "no source of funding would be acceptable to ACSH's critics. What our critics object to is not our funding, but our conclusions."

Accountability and Balancing the Human Ecosystem

By pointing out that advocates are neither infallible nor motiveless, I do not mean to imply that they are unworthy participants in the public domain. Advocates are an essential species in the ecology of American political life. In our raucous democracy, where a messenger of bad news usually is removed from office at the next election, it rarely makes political sense for elected leaders to propose solutions to a problem until faced with a crisis. By their narrow-issue focus, advocates are highly effective at creating crises, getting media attention, and whipping up action.

As natural predators, advocates also help keep the political process honest. If a government agency or a corporation suppresses information or self-servingly distorts research, advocates swoop in and inform the public. We gain a more accurate view of the facts through the advocates' information-gathering acumen and adroit use of mass communications.

Yet the fact that advocates have the power to influence the course of critical issues on which there is no scientific or political consensus reveals an imbalance in the political ecosystem. The implication that indifferent governance and unscrupulous business are to blame for society's problems

97

reflects a pervasive distrust of the very institutions intended to protect it. The advocates themselves foster some of this distrust by impugning the motives and actions of their critics in government, courts, scientific establishments, and industry.

And examples abound that show the questionable activities practiced by these institutions. Are we to trust the predictions of a government that could not foresee the savings and loan debacle or that provided false information to the defense department by the CIA? Should we put our trust in its vision? Should we put our planet's future in its hands? Can we trust scientific establishments that pander to those who fund them, courts that issue findings based on flawed information, or industries that pay to manipulate the legislators?

Without effective counterweights in the institutions representing the public's interests, the only way to balance the scale is to demand accountability from everyone, including the advocates. Advocates are not prophets. They are not arbiters of right and wrong. They espouse political positions. They have interests to protect and goals to achieve.

No advocate or expert can give answers to the major questions of our day, no matter how strongly they argue. They cannot even tell us where individual responsibility ends and corporate fault begins. They cannot even tell us whether cloth diapers or disposable diapers are better for our planet. They are merely part of a collective process from which we draw conclusions as best we can, subject always to current knowledge and human fallibility.

Facing Up to the Risk Equation

Admitting to our fear of fallibility and vulnerability makes it easy for us to accept the advocates' definitive answers. It is up to us—easy to say, difficult to do—to resist the advocates' appeals to our fear of the future and our abhorrence of risk.

We will never be free of risk. Every action, no matter how insignificant, has a risk. According to the National Safety Council, 102,397 people were injured by their own clothing and 43,868 were injured by their jewelry last year. Nobody argues that we should do away with clothing and jewelry.

Risk is measured on a balance sheet. If we take an action that someone says will save a species, or a forest, or a life, we must calculate the costs of our choice. In taking such action we must recognize we will never have all the information we need: the earth is far more complex than our technologies are for investigating and describing it. We must accept that sometimes we will act in error; fallibility is our fate as human beings.

There are always choices to be made, particularly when a human good appears to conflict with an ecological aim. For example, the Pacific yew, found in the old-growth forests of the Northwest, is the source of an anticancer drug called taxol. Some people fear that harvesting the Pacific yew will hasten the forest's demise, threatening the extinction of the northern spotted owl and other species. For patients with advanced cancer, however, taxol has shown remarkable efficacy. Which is the greater good? And more to the point, who should be making the decision?

The process of making a choice is less comfortable when the human impact is economic, not health-related. Thousands of loggers in the Northwest will be out of work when the U.S. Department of the Interior designates certain sections of the old-growth forests as protected habitats. Which is the greater cost: the damage to the human ecology of the Northwest or the damage to these forests? How do

99

we find the most effective compromise to serve both interests?

Decisions about the use of new technologies also call for informed choices. Many of the technologies taken for granted today were treated with the same skepticism that greeted nuclear power plants. For example, it took fifty years for the general public to regard commercial canning as safe, although commercially canned food caused less food poisoning than home-preserved food.

Even the most bizarre technologies can lead to important and unforeseen human benefits. The same nuclear age that gave us the atom bomb also gave us nuclear medicine, a technology that makes it possible to diagnose and treat diseases earlier with noninvasive procedures and less pain and risk. It is tempting to believe, as people of the Middle Ages did, that there is one right use of the earth, one correct answer to every dilemma. But despite the certainties of advocates, few issues are likely to have a single acceptable solution, and few solutions are likely to come with a guarantee.

Global Hubris

Particularly in our relation to the environment, perspective is all-important. The earth is four and a half billion years old. If that life span were represented by one day, human beings would have appeared less than thirty seconds before midnight. We modern humans with our industrialized, fossil-fuel-fired civilization would have appeared in just a fraction of the last second.

How much or how little damage have we done to this planet in our short lifespan? None of us knows. We can and should strive to live less wastefully and more frugally. But even those terms are not absolute. No one can lay claim to a formula that tells whether saving the snail darter or building the dam would better serve the greater good.

Our intellectual pride does not allow us to imagine that our world functions by principles that remain utterly beyond our control or comprehension. Some of us take a perverse comfort in arguing over who is killing the world fastest.

I think a character in the book *Jurassic Park* best addresses the failures and shortsightedness of experts—in this case environmental experts—when he responds to questions about the threat of radiation, depletion of ozone, and preservation of the environment, by saying:

> Our planet is four and a half billion years old. There has been life on this planet for nearly that long. . . . The evolutionary process would begin again . . . the earth would survive . . . life would survive. . . . Only we think it wouldn't. . . . The planet is not in jeopardy. We are in jeopardy. We haven't got the power to destroy the planet—or to save it. But we might have the power to save ourselves.

I, like the character in *Jurassic Park*, am far less concerned about the earth, and more concerned about the human condition and the innumerable ways we poison the seconds, minutes, and hours of our precious days. The strident certainties of advocates, far from enhancing the human environment, deposit toxic waste in our intellectual veins. The conditions from which advocacy gains its momentum—particularly governmental untrustworthiness and scientific querulousness—are a spiritual landfill whose odor is so much a part of our everyday world that we can no longer smell the decay.

101

Chapter 6

Power of Prognostication

> A woman who mistakenly believed the celebrated astron-
> omer Sir Isaac Newton was an astrologer visited him
> repeatedly and insisted he find her lost purse. Unable to
> rid himself of her any other way, Sir Isaac finally agreed
> to help. Drawing a chalk circle around himself, he mum-
> bled mysterious-sounding invocations, then told her to
> look for her purse near Greenwich Hospital, on the
> lawn under the third front window. The woman did as
> Newton said—and found her purse.
>
> *—Little, Brown Book of Anecdotes*

This apocryphal story is a wry testament to our faith in the
power of prognostication. Our faith stems from a belief
that scientists have access to the inner meaning of reality
through objective experimentation and the ability to quan-
tify what they find.

For many people, numbers hold little more meaning than
an astrologer's fanciful incantations. A large part of the
population, when asked about their proficiency in mathe-
matics, confessed that they were not "number people."
They believe they cannot understand numbers and statistics,
so they invest in the incantations of those who purport to
unravel the mysteries of the universe: the scientists.

The mystery of numbers has the magical power to sus-

103

pend doubt and inspire belief. Many of us expect scientists to use these magical tools to find the things we have somehow lost: our certainty, our confidence about the future, our means for building a societywide consensus to cope with the problems that face our nation. And so some of us are dangerously susceptible when a scientist, social scientist, or any expert shows us numbers calculated by a purportedly objective process and declares them to be true indicators of the best and healthiest ways for us to live.

Because we want to believe that someone has the answers to all of our questions, we are tempted to suspend our responsibility and to let the prognosticators tell us what to do. We have become a credulous aspect of society. Like Newton's persistent visitor who confused science with superstition, many people—even scientists themselves—confuse numbers with truth, trends with predictions, methodology with objectivity, correlations with cause.

Mythology of Science

Many of us have a rudimentary familiarity with the scientific method. As children we learn that science is a way of discovering new information about the world through direct observation. We are taught that science performs these observations objectively. Even though a scientific experiment begins with a speculation or hypothesis about the outcome, the goal of scientific experimentation is not the outcome, but the truth.

To a child, the idea of testing reality without having a particular goal in mind sounds highly plausible. Children themselves are natural scientists. When a baby plays with matches, for example, his goal is not to light a fire but to find out what these funny-smelling sticks can do. When children open a cabinet and pull out everything inside, they are experiencing the pure joy of discovery.

Most people's view of science is colored by their visceral memory of this pleasurable and uncomplicated state of learning. Even people who study science as adults often maintain a childlike belief in the objectivity of science and in its ability to sort out the confused messages of the world to find truth.

The basic tenet of science is objectivity. In tests of new drugs, for example, biomedical researchers use "double-blind" studies so that neither the study participants nor the investigators knows who is getting the real treatment and who is getting the placebo. Double-blinding is meant to insulate studies from the expectations of those involved and from self-fulfilling prophecies: For example, the possibility that study participants may consciously or unconsciously try to please the researchers by espousing the desired response; and the expectations of the investigators themselves, who may consciously or unconsciously try to influence the study's outcome to prove their hypothesis.

Double-blinding is one of the procedures that makes science appear "scientific" to everyone, including scientists themselves. But procedures like double-blinding are ultimately part of the mythology of science—the powerful belief system that puts science purportedly above the motivations of the human heart.

Even if scientists were not motivated like the rest of us by personal needs and goals, science by its very nature cannot be "objective" or "goal-less." Confirming a theory by observation requires the experimenter to devise procedures that will favor the theory's plausibility. Research on *anything* will yield findings that are a reflection of, and limited by, its procedures for observing or measuring.

This principle is simple to understand. If I am color-

105

blind and want to paint a picture of an autumn landscape, for example, my painting will lack the distinctive red hues that characterize certain maple trees. If I am quickly sorting change in my pocket by size and color, I may not notice that I have several Canadian pennies or dimes among my American pennies and dimes. Both of these deviations from "objective reality" are not malicious: in one case, I am prevented from seeing what I miss, and in the other, I simply am not interested in the distinctions. These are what I call "inherent biases": they are not malicious but merely part of the limits of observation.

Understanding the typical blind spots and inattentiveness of the scientific experts is critical. Science will always have a role to play in interpreting the world, but not the role of a soothsayer.

Trends or Truth?

The desire to see proof in trends is an ancient human trait. Human beings have always felt there were secret meanings in coincidences. If the rain came when a chant was sung at sunset, for example, our ancestors believed chanting brought the rain.

Children are notorious for misjudging cause and effect. I know a family whose youngest child insisted on visiting the restroom in every restaurant they went to. It became a family joke that the child had been in every bathroom in town. Tired of being teased, the little girl explained that she went to the restroom not because she needed to, but because when she returned to the table her food was always there. She believed that her absence from the table caused the food to arrive.

Unlike the little girl's approach, the experts believe that

quantitative research in the sciences is a more sophisticated way of looking for meaningful coincidences. Powerful computers add to the mystique of statistical correlations by evaluating every quantifiable variable in an experiment or research project and calculating the results to as many decimal places as desired. Often those results are accompanied by more numbers announcing the "statistical significance" and "confidence factor" for each conclusion reached.

Albeit, these impressive numbers still only represent correlations: coincident facts that may or may not be related. Because a basic characteristic of our minds is the tendency to recognize and recall facts about things we already know, the statistical correlations that interest us tell more about ourselves and our preoccupations than they do about the subjects we study.

For example, when several studies found that young drug experimenters in the 1960s and 1970s tended to use alcohol before they used drugs, researchers concluded that experimentation with alcohol leads to experimentation with drugs. The conclusion seems obvious because we are predisposed to believe it. We could just as well conclude that daily use of alcohol leads to financial well-being, since a study of Harvard's class of 1940 showed that those who drank every day had higher incomes than occasional drinkers or nondrinkers. Based solely on the data, we have no idea whether daily drinking has anything to do with income status. Similarly, we have no idea whether the prior use of alcohol had anything to do with the subsequent use of drugs.

Our minds are biologically programmed to recognize and complete patterns. For this reason, we are more likely to pay attention to numbers that correspond to an existing belief system. For example, the National Academy of Sciences (NAS) used a study showing higher rates of lung-cancer deaths among nonsmokers who lived with smokers to come up with an estimate of 3,800 lung-cancer deaths annually caused by passive smoking. Since it has already been established that active smoking causes some lung cancer, the conclusion about passive smoking seemed easy to accept.

But I later learned that the study did not take into account participants' exposure to radon, a naturally produced gas and the deadliest known environmental carcinogen. Radon is believed to cause 20,000 lung-cancer deaths annually. So despite the plausibility of NAS's conclusions, they can't be relied on: radon may have caused some or all of those 3,800 deaths. Many other variables—obvious and measurable, not-so-obvious and unmeasurable—can cause or prevent lung cancer.

For many years, the tobacco industry argued that there was no *proof* that cigarette smoking caused lung cancer— just statistical correlations. The industry's argument was deemed self-serving and false: there was strong test-tube evidence that the chemicals in cigarette smoke could initiate cancerous changes in lung tissue. Yet their insistence that the demographic and statistical data did not prove anything was absolutely correct.

The statistical analysis was highly suggestive and pointed researchers in the right direction, but it did not prove—and still does not prove—that cigarette smoking by itself causes lung cancer. As a matter of fact, the *Harvard Health Letter* of August 1995 reports that 85 percent of smokers *never* (emphasis added) develop lung cancer.

Methodology and Outcome Control

Interpreting correlations through expectations is not the only source of inherent bias in science. In some cases, like the sorting of pocket change by size and color, the method of observation chosen misses crucial information or implies that conclusions are more reliable than they actually are.

On the simplest level, for example, researchers and public opinion pollsters can word their questions carefully to control the type of responses received. One study, for example, found that 44 percent of people questioned would agree to a risky treatment for lung cancer if told it would give them a 68 percent chance of surviving. But when the researchers restated the question and presented the risks of the same treatment as a 32 percent chance of dying, only 18 percent said they would undergo the treatment.

The same principle of controlled questions can be used in a study design. A recent study, for example, found that women who took two drinks a day were found to be more than three times as likely to die before age sixty-five as abstainers. Researchers used death certificates to select study participants. They then worked backward from the stated cause of death, interviewing family members to find out information about each deceased woman's drinking habits.

At least two possible sources of error can be found in this methodology. First, the cause of death as listed on a death certificate often is incomplete, inaccurate, or both. Second, people's recollections about their own (or others') past drinking habits are notoriously unreliable. By the numbers alone, the study ostensibly proved its hypothesis that moderate drinking is bad for health. Yet the methodological failings render the study's conclusions meaningless.

Such power to control variables gives ample room for an expert's biases and expectations to affect the outcome of research. Studies that receive extensive press coverage and are offered as scientific proof by experts may have similarly invalidating flaws.

Whenever data is interpreted, subject bias operates. For example, two trained and experienced radiologists will look at the same X ray and reach different conclusions. Examples are legion of this sort of subjective interpretation. In 1990, for example, a team of researchers reported it had discovered evidence of an "alcoholism gene." They claimed to have found a gene that caused organic differences between the brains of alcoholic people and nonalcoholic people.

The press accounts rarely mentioned that the researchers' methodology was unusual in the field of genetic research. Normally, a genetic researcher investigates the family histories of all study subjects to look for evidence of a family predisposition to alcoholism. The researchers, however, did not do family studies. They used instead a sophisticated method of tissue analysis to compare the brain tissue of people who died of alcoholism with that of people who did not.

Paul Billings, director of the Clinic for Inherited Disease at New England Deaconess Hospital, interviewed by the *New Republic* about the study, said tissue analysis without family studies is meaningless. "If this type of genetic analysis was carried out for a disease or a behavior less attractive than alcoholism, it would never get published," said Billings. "It tells you nothing of significance." Billings's statement is crucial: the more emotional the subject, the more likely the experts' questionable conclusions will be bought by the public.

A later study suggested another methodological problem with the alcoholism gene findings. For example, the gene in question, the researchers note, appears more often in some racial and ethnic groups than others. To eliminate race as a possible source of confusion, these researchers limited their study only to Caucasian subjects. The researchers found no statistically significant difference between the

110

number of alcoholic and nonalcoholic people in the study group who carried the gene.

Scientists and other experts find tissue analysis and other high-tech methods attractive because they deal exclusively with quantitative data, such as the number and types of cells present in the brain. By taking a subject, particularly an emotionally charged subject as noted above, they hope to achieve a clean, uncomplicated objectivity. The benefit of the method, however, is precisely its limitation. *You can't take the human and personal elements out of behavior*, and these are not measurable.

The same fundamental problem occurred in the recently announced discovery of a biological difference between heterosexual and homosexual men. Again through tissue studies, researcher Simon LeVay announced that he had found one node of the hypothalamus to be larger in heterosexual men than in homosexual men. The hypothalamus is a primitive part of the brain that, among its functions, regulates sexual behavior; in homosexual men, LeVay said, the node's size is similar to that found in women.

LeVay obtained the brain tissue used in his research from autopsies of forty-one people who died at hospitals in New York and California. Nineteen were homosexual men who died of complications of AIDS; sixteen were "presumed" heterosexual men, six of whom were intravenous drug users who also died of AIDS; and six were heterosexual women, one of whom died of AIDS.

Many researchers criticized the study for its use of AIDS patients, whose brains are affected in as-yet unknown ways by the virus. But the fundamental problem is that studying brain cells under a microscope cannot tell you anything meaningful about human sexuality. Sexuality is a complex mix of drives, desires, fantasies, and behaviors. Some people with homosexual desires, for example, may only express them in their fantasy lives. Without access to clarifying information from the people in the study, the comparisons are meaningless.

The more emotionally charged a subject, the more likely it is that results achieved by objective-sounding methodologies such as brain tissue analysis will be attractive as ways of "objectively" proving the point. But without information from the brain's owner, the physiological structures of the brain are no more enlightening about human behavior than phrenology—the practice of judging personality through the bumps on a person's head. The experts' quantitative methodology does not guarantee objectivity, particularly when human behavior is the subject matter being quantified.

Constraints on Inquiry

Because science is so commonly idealized, many scientists develop a paternalistic attitude about the public's ability to weigh evidence and make informed decisions. In the field of alcohol research, for example, are people who believe science had to control the flow of information to protect society from itself and its own actions to forestall some dreaded end. I saw this process many times when I headed NIAAA, but never more so than in the controversy over the release of the 1976 RAND Report.

At that time, the RAND Corporation was evaluating the alcoholism treatment centers that our agency had set up around the country. They were examining the effectiveness of treatment. In the course of their examination, the RAND researchers noted that a small minority of alcoholic people had returned to social drinking after treatment without experiencing a recurrence of their former drinking problem.

112

The finding, little more than an interesting aside to the principal function of the report, unleashed a whirlwind of response within and outside government. As I discussed in chapter 3, the predominant philosophy in the field, central to AA and other alcoholism treatment programs, is once an alcoholic, always an alcoholic. As a result of this belief, a finding that went against the belief became a powerful threat to believers. I immediately felt pressure to quash the report. Some of my advisory board members were convinced that releasing of the report would cause thousands of alcoholic people to return to drink. One board member, who was also on the board of the RAND Corporation, put enormous pressure on RAND to withdraw the report.

The RAND Report was released with its conclusions intact. A second study confirmed the findings of the first study. No evidence exists that alcoholic people returned to alcohol as an outcome of the report's release. I can't help but think that, if someone had been in charge who shared that belief system, the RAND Report might simply have disappeared—and it would not have been the first government study to do so.

The people who argued for suppressing the RAND data were not unkind people; they never thought of themselves as trying to manipulate the public. They were sincerely concerned that alcoholic people would uncritically react to the report and start drinking again. In that context, they saw nothing wrong with suppressing information; they saw it as their duty as guardians of the public welfare.

A similar logic governs the virtual suppression of information about the health benefits of moderate drinking. Researchers have repeatedly found that men who drink one or two drinks a day are much less likely to die of heart attacks than either nondrinkers or heavy drinkers. Those who drink an average of one drink a day are less likely to

113

die of all other major causes, such as cancer, stroke, and accidents. With heart disease still the number one killer overall in the United States, it is surprising that these findings are not discussed more widely in prevention literature.

So great is the fear of alcohol's power and so great the fear of subtle seductions to drink that positive health findings involving alcohol are all but ignored. The American Medical Association, not known as a friend of the alcohol industry, has written that if the United States became totally abstinent, there would be 81,000 more cardiac deaths every year on average. Another study reports better cognition in older people who are moderate drinkers than in non-drinkers.

In some cases, the paternalistic desire to protect the public becomes a form of censorship that works to enshrine the view of the censor. Enoch Gordis, M.D., the current director of NIAAA, says his agency receives few grant applications to study the potential beneficial effects of alcohol, "although," he says,"it is a researchable topic."

Within scientific disciplines, the pressure for conformity to preserve the status quo can be enormous. I learned this lesson the first time I served on a grant-review committee. I did not think that the considered proposal was worth supporting. The committee chairman supported the grant and had enough votes on the committee to approve it, but he wanted unanimity. He made it plain to me in subtle ways that if I did not agree, I would be excluded from participating in grant reviews in the future. I changed my vote. Ironically, I never was called on to serve by that man again.

Although I had compromised my principles to ingratiate myself, my initial dissent posed too great a risk of nonconformity. Ostracism or marginalization by one's peers, especially in a field dominated by "experts," is the ultimate weapon to ensure conformity. Nearly anyone, whatever their stature, can be effectively intimidated by the threat of ostracism. Sigmund Freud, for example, originally proposed in 1896 that the neurotic symptoms reported by so many of his female patients resulted from sexual abuse suffered in childhood.

Standard psychoanalytic history has it that Freud changed his mind about this conclusion, eventually realizing that these traumatic memories were actually fantasies arising from unconscious wishes. Historian Jeffrey Moussaieff Masson contends that Freud did not change his mind. Masson believes Freud feared his colleagues would ostracize him for attributing such ugly behavior to so many men of the upper class.

Freud had reason to fear such censure. A French physician, Ambrose Tardieu, had been ruined when he made a similar suggestion in 1850; and a follower of Freud, Sandor Ferenczi, was hounded out of the psychoanalytic community when he raised the same possibility in 1933.

Power of Expectation

The promises of the [scientist] are like those of the astrologers, who boast that they can foretell future things, and do not even know the present or the past. . . . I do not know whether their fraud is more shameful, or our folly in believing, as we do.
—Giulia Gonzaga, c. 1550

Human frailties and the inherent biases in observation limit the reliability of the scientific expert as prognosticator. When scientists become involved in public policy issues, their pronouncements are no more reliable than any advocate. And when scientists predict the future, their predictions are no more likely to be right than those of astrologers.

115

An example of the difficulties in translating scientific knowledge into predictions occurred in 1975, when highway safety experts tried to predict the rate of fatal accidents in the next decade. They predicted that highway fatalities would rise from 40,000 in 1975 to 72,300 in 1985. But by 1985, highway fatalities had declined slightly to 39,300. In 1994, with more cars and drivers on the road, traffic fatalities were 40,400.

The experts had factored in every variable they knew of that could affect safety. They quantified the effects of more driving, more drinking, more speeding, and smaller cars; they took into account automobile safety improvements and the rate of deterioration of highway surfaces. As it turned out, none of these variables showed any significant relation to the highway fatality rate.

Studying the problem with the benefit of hindsight, one researcher noted three factors that seemed to match state-to-state differences in the fatal accident rate: the percentage of drivers under twenty-five, the rate of death from nontraffic accidents, and each state's homicide rate. The lower these variables were, the lower the state's accident rate. And we cannot be sure that even these variables are the whole story.

This experience demonstrates how much more complex human behavior is than any set of variables we can control for in our quantitative methodologies. It would have taken the wisdom of a philosopher, not the methods of a statistician, to predict that the rate of fatal automobile accidents perhaps reflects a society's reverence for life, not its engineering achievements or safety improvements.

Because of the inordinate credibility assigned to scientific predictions, the great danger is that these prognostications may become self-fulfilling prophecies, contributing to the problems they are supposed to help us avoid. A recent report from the National Institutes of Health, for example, suggests that because physicians, nurses, and others in the health-care field believe that growing older means an increase in sickness and frailty, they fail to provide the latest in treatment and preventive care, actually causing more debility among the elderly.

Another danger to prognostication and the tyranny of experts is that the general public's emotional responses to frightening statistics may lead legislators to adopt policies with unintended outcomes as bad or worse than the original problem. The public pressure to reduce the frightening statistics on drug use and street crime, for example, has led to unprecedented pressure on police officers. Some of them crack under the pressure, exploding with rage and violence against the drug suspects they arrest.

In Dayton, Ohio, for example, a well-respected police officer was accused of torturing a handcuffed drug suspect with a hot iron while interrogating him. Some police officers blamed the war on drugs, not lingering racism, for the repugnant show of force captured on videotape in Los Angeles showing police officers savagely beating Rodney King, an unarmed black man.

Some of us are poorly equipped to challenge the power of the experts' statistics and their supposedly objective problem-solving skills. For example, among 170 million adult Americans, 27 million read below the fifth-grade level. Some 60 to 65 million read below the ninth grade level. To comprehend the public policy discussions on the op-ed pages of the *New York Times*, the *Washington Post*, or the *Wall Street Journal*, a reader needs at least a twelfth-grade reading level. In other words, nearly two out of five Americans are ill-equipped to participate fully in public life. They do not have the resources available to them should they wish to question the scientists and would-be prognosticators.

Even the highly educated lack basic knowledge of science and technology—information vital to public discussion of issues facing us in the 1990s. In 1987, for example, a filmmaker at Harvard's commencement asked twenty-three students why summer is hotter than winter. Only two answered correctly. The rest did not know that the angle of the sun (its solstice or equinox) determines how much or how little heat the earth receives.

When a geophysicist and a physicist at a scientific seminar asked twenty-four of their colleagues to explain the difference between DNA and RNA, the two basic building blocks of molecular genetics, only three knew the answer (RNA and DNA are nucleic acids. RNA helps to control cellular chemical activities, while DNA is the basis of heredity).

When highly educated people do not know the basic principles of science, they too will surrender to the expert-fed preoccupations discussed throughout this book: obsession with risk; panic over imagined disasters; need to control others' decisions; compulsion to confess behavioral weaknesses; zeal to identify and protect victims; belief in scientific objectivity; and doubt in ourselves. These behaviors are related to addiction in the way they lure the vulnerable.

I believe we are especially vulnerable to manipulation when it comes to children. Why do some parents and adults go beyond the norm in trying to save the children? It's because they themselves feel flawed, and a ready excuse for flaws is to blame someone or something for letting them down. What better compensatory mechanism for their defects than to save and protect the children.

Advocates zealously monitor children's exposure to nudity, violence, promotions on pleasure, and the like, because children see the truths adults don't want them to see. Over one hundred years ago, Hans Christian Anderson in his fable "The Emperor's New Clothes" made this telling point. As a result of overprotection, many of the problems they visit on their children are the problems they never solved in themselves.

A teenager wrote to the *New York Times* on 5 August, 1995: "You also portray teenagers as ignorant flakes. . . . I know plenty of smokers, none of whom are naive about the dangers of smoking. America's youth of today are more informed about the dangers of tobacco than the young in the 1950's or 60's. In general, teenagers know the dangers of most of their activities, but to the horror of our parents, we choose to take the risks and do what we want anyway."

While we occupy ourselves with causes or celebrities, the disease of the week, the crisis of the month, or the balm of a new *ism*, our social systems are going to hell in a hand basket: the savings and loan debacle, the national debt of trillions of dollars, cities unable to afford proper education and proper health care.

"By delusions of apparent good," said Niccolò Machiavelli in the 1520s, "the people are often misled to desire their own ruin." When statistics and quantitative models do our thinking and feeling for us, and when we become so cowed by the power of numbers that we abdicate our responsibilities to the experts who wield them, then we are likely to get a chaotic society.

Phony-Baloney Factor

In 1989 and 1990, Milli Vanilli, a rock duo, sold hundreds of thousands of copies of their debut album and

119

received one of the music industry's highest honors, the Grammy Award for Best New Artist—all without being able to sing a note. In live performances, the duo lip-synched to vocals recorded by two anonymous singers.

The most telling irony of the Milli Vanilli incident is how the duo was finally exposed: they themselves lost track of what was real. When a second album was about to be cut, they decided to do their own singing. Their vocal talents were so meager, however, that their producer decided the wiser course was to expose the fraud.

Milli Vanilli is a cultural icon of what columnist Joel Achenbach calls the "phony-baloney factor": the frequency with which we are taken in by people who are not what they seem and who often forget what's real.

The overvaluation of statistics and the appearance of objectivity may be the most pervasive examples of the phony-baloney factor in the United States in the 1990s. The aura of certainty and prognostication in a tumultuous, rapidly changing society feed on belief.

Relinquishing the comfort of numbers means relinquishing our hope of certainty. We won't give up that hope easily. It goes to the core of our being, as the child who covets order and predictability and as the adult who fears the certainty of death.

Scientists themselves have a powerful emotional drive to believe their work generates eternal, incontrovertible truths. Albert Einstein was terribly disturbed when, as a result of his theories of relativity, physicists proposed that the subatomic universe could only be described by statistical probability, not fundamental and immutable physical law. "God," wrote Einstein in 1926, "does not play dice with the universe." He spent the rest of his career searching for a theory that would replace chance with certainty.

Although some people believe Americans are too disinterested in science and statistics or too dazed by television to critically examine the world around them, I believe nearly all of us are capable of seeing through science's self-aggrandizement.

If we are to live sanely in a phony-baloney world of scientific predictions, the need to see clearly is far more important than clear sight itself. We must begin with an understanding that truth is not within the purview of science, but of faith. Science protects us from our biases and credulities as we try to understand our world. The business of science is like the business of life—a perilous endeavor in which uncertainty, not certainty, is the likely course.

Chapter 7

Life beyond Advice

No lesson seems to be so deeply inculcated by the experience of life as that you should never trust experts. If you believe the doctors, nothing is wholesome; if you believe the theologians, nothing is innocent; if you believe the soldiers, nothing is safe. They all require to have their strong wine diluted by a very large admixture of common sense.

—Robert, Lord Salisbury (1877)

All professions are conspiracies against the laity.

—George Bernard Shaw,
The Doctor's Dilemma (1906)

An expert is one who knows more and more about less and less.

—Nicholas Murray Butler, U.S. educator,
1931 winner of the Nobel Peace Prize

In my research for this book, I was struck by the existence of a long tradition of warnings not to take experts seriously. That tradition helps me keep my perspective, particularly when somber thoughts trouble me. Our age is not unique in being beset by a glut of advisers; and surely we, like the generations before us, will survive their advice.

I also keep my balance by recalling a lesson I learned from my friend and mentor, Norbert Wiener, who epito-

123

mized why experts frequently outsmart themselves by their narrow focus. Norbert was a true genius, but I always beat him at chess. He focused so completely on his area of expertise—his own plans and moves—that he failed to take into account my play and the possible outcome of my moves.

Although intelligence and knowledge are authentic human treasures, they do not guarantee that their possessors will always be right. Sometimes our own intelligence and knowledge can so befuddle our natural instincts that we wind up making ludicrous mistakes. In this regard, I like to think about Hans Christian Anderson's "The Emperor's New Clothes." In this story, the adults stand by cheering as their emperor parades through the streets in his "new clothes." The adults know that the emperor is naked, but they are too respectful to say anything. Finally a child, too young to be awed by greatness, exclaims, "But he has nothing on!"

The child comes to this conclusion using not information or knowledge but common sense. His elders, however, let cowardice belie their common sense and wind up looking like fools.

When I hear the din of experts who daily try to instruct us on how to think and how to live, I try to keep that child's clear voice in mind as he separated fantasy from reality. I believe each of us possesses a native wisdom to live in the world as it really is and to master the tools needed to build an honest, healthy, wholesome life.

Are There Answers?

The experts I have chosen to focus my attention on throughout this book are my own shadows. As a physician,

124

psychiatrist, scientist, authority on alcoholism treatment, social engineer, advocate of the disenfranchised, and political animal to my core, these are the people with whom I have worked—whose expert status I have shared, and whose deceptions and self-deceptions I comprehend. Collectively, their portraits are for me a chastening hall of mirrors. As I review the petty ambitions, the blind spots, the frightening lack of self-knowledge, I may see my own face staring back at me.

Nonetheless, I believe these people deserve the special attention I have paid them, because they are the experts whose claims we must critically examine to defend ourselves. Through their emotional appeals to our childlike wishes for unequivocal answers to frightening questions, they worm themselves and their agendas into the deepest, most vulnerable recesses of our psyches. Once inside, they can render us traitors to ourselves. We want the answers they promise at any price, even while we're uneasy about their motives or methods.

Experts gain ascendancy when they exploit our vulnerability to easy answers. In areas of technical or factual competence, experts generally have answers superior to those of the lay person. For instance, if I want my car fixed, I'll go to a trained mechanic rather than to my neighbor.

On the other hand, when experts predict the future or tell me how to live, I would be leary of their advice. Hard as it is to accept, there are no answers. And in such matters, there is no guarantee that the expert will be any more knowledgeable than my neighbor. Even the most brilliant experts cannot accurately predict future outcomes. I recall a talk by a geologist at the Aspen Institute in 1973, complete with impressive charts and tables, showing that the world would be out of oil by 1985.

When experts venture into the realm of prediction or

prescription, they are no longer relying solely on their specialized knowledge. Their advice is qualified by their values, their blind spots, and their inability to consider all possible factors. Thomas Malthus, for example, based his infamous calculations of the number of people the world's agricultural land could support on a formula that presumed the productive acres needed to feed the world's horses. The world found a substitute for horses.

In their rush to provide the world with answers, experts often make the same mistake my friend Norbert did when playing chess: they focus so narrowly on the logic of their disciplines that they forget to consider the unpredictable. The debate over capital punishment, for example, is couched in objective-sounding arguments, but actually reflects the perspective of the advocates. Both those who argue for capital punishment and those who argue against it share the common premise that there is no greater punishment than death. But they neglect to ask a very pertinent question: Does the violent criminal share this belief? As a psychiatrist, I know that not everyone puts self-preservation above all other values. Hopelessness, depression, a sense of futility, and low self-esteem make life cheap. If we want to change the behavior of violent criminals, we have to understand their behavior not ours.

But we cannot castigate the experts if we choose to abdicate our judgment. Every one of us at one time or another has abused our influence over a situation or person, even though we knew it was wrong. But we did it anyway. Unless we are willing to take responsibility for informing ourselves, voicing our opinions, and making our own decisions, we invite the experts' free reign.

Standing up for ourselves and making our own decisions is not an easy task. In today's world the pressure to abdicate personal responsibility in exchange for simple answers to complex problems is stronger than ever. For instance, we find it much easier to believe the prevailing convention that a war on drugs will cure violent crime than to consider the far more complex and less comforting reality.

Rather than looking for the causes of violence in the cinematic images of the drug culture, we might well ask ourselves whether decades of poverty, chronic unemployment, inadequate education, dilapidated housing, poor health care, a lack of public services, and an apathetic political bureaucracy might bear any of the burden of responsibility. Then we might well ask what we, as individuals, plan to do about these problems. And how we, as part of this society, plan to get others to help.

Working out solutions is our responsibility as citizens and concerned human beings. If we delegate that responsibility to the experts, we lose our opportunity to build the world we desire.

Benefits of Diversity

Throughout this book, I've tried to make it clear that no matter what experts promise, there will never be a pill, mechanism, or formula to solve personal or social ills. Rather, authentic solutions will be born in a crucible where differing and competing ideas are commingled.

Our world must be made safe for democracy—not democracy as the governmental form to which President Woodrow Wilson was referring when he made this observation in 1917, but the democracy of ideas, the rough-and-tumble of discourse among people who respect each other's rights to express themselves and to hold differing opinions.

The quest for simple answers and a one-size-fits-all solution to social problems homogenizes intellectual inquiry.

The ever-present fear among researchers of displeasing those who hold the purse strings and the lure of ink and airtime available to a scientific-sounding anyone on a headline-worthy subject subvert the process of original thinking and discourage dissent.

In the world of nature, our renewed appreciation for the intricacies of ecological balance—a legacy of environmental advocacy—reminds us that a diverse species is a precious, nonrenewable resource. Similarly, we must learn to live with people who hold views different from our own, accepting their ideas as evidence of the diversity of the human spirit.

Dissent in intellectual inquiry, in politics, in academia, in business, and in family life is part of the ecological balance of human society. The American Museum of Natural History, for example, includes in its exhibit catalog a synopsis of scientific debate about its controversial new exhibit, a fifty-five-foot *Barosaurus* rearing back in a manner some say is an unlikely pose. The goal of these unusual catalog notes, according to the museum's curators, is to help people understand that disagreements are a healthy, normal part of the work of science.

When science or any human endeavor tries to sanitize dissent, it robs us all of crucial information about the process by which decisions are made and new knowledge is learned. It prevents us from seeing that false starts, partial truths, and the laborious accumulation of hard-to-evaluate data are a part of the processes of inquiry.

It is up to each of us to demand intellectual honesty of the experts who surround us. In return, we must accept without flinching that these figures, whom we idealize, are neither perfect nor infallible. Tolerating plurality of opinion or ambiguity of conclusions is not a confession of failure: it is the price we pay for being human, and not gods.

128

Integrative Function

Accepting diversity does not mean surrendering to chaos. Each of us is uniquely gifted with a means of making sense of diversity. Each of us has the capacity to filter, sift, and combine bits of information into an integrated whole greater than the sum of its parts. This process is called integrative thinking.

Expertise isolates facts from their human context and renders them as concrete equations. Integrative thinking, however, resists this tendency toward concreteness and is comfortable with abstractions. It resists the kind of thinking found in single-issue politics, where the politician has no vision of the whole picture. It resists the corporate bottom-line watchers who are more interested in their company's short-term profits than in its long-term stability and growth.

We are all by nature integrative thinkers, regardless of our education or status in life. Some years ago, I took part in a seminar in which a group of ordinary people of various ages and backgrounds were given a complex engineering problem to solve. Although the group included many highly educated people, including a professional engineer, a housewife, and a landscape architect came up with the solution.

Japan's quality circles, emulated in some U.S. companies where workers evolve solutions, are an excellent example of the integrative function in action. DuPont's gunpowder manufacturing division, famous for its safety record, uses a similar idea. Instead of sending safety experts around to lecture people on safety, the company trains its foremen to hold safety conferences with workers. The discourse is two-way, with workers contributing their perspectives and ideas.

129

In the process, everyone learns to think ahead to make a dangerous environment safer and more efficient.

Such efforts reinforce the dignity and confidence of the individual. They acknowledge that we are all experts when it comes to thinking about our jobs, our families, and our lives. Many well-known experts, in fact, started with no special knowledge of the field they entered. They are ordinary people who found a successful solution to a personal problem and hark back to it as a formula for others. Weight-loss experts Richard Simmons and Jenny Craig, for example, were themselves overweight.

Even AA and its many offsprings are, at heart, solutions to the personal problems of Dr. Bob Smith and Bill Wilson. When faced with our own crises, we would do well to emulate the creativity of these people rather than investing all our hopes in following solutions that worked for others.

Using the integrative function is an essential exercise of an individual's identity. As muscles in an arm atrophy when immobilized in a cast, so will our identity atrophy if we submit to the will of others. When we don't express ourselves, we will cease to have a firm sense of self and seek identity in a diagnosis or a cause.

A person with a strong sense of self is more resourceful even in the most dismal of circumstances. Art collector and medical publisher Arthur Sackler, for example, was a creative genius at turning negative outcomes into lucky breaks. He made his fortune in the pharmaceutical industry by studying the adverse effects of drugs and determining their positive use in medicine.

Creative, skilled, spirited people in full possession of their integrative powers are the world's most valuable natural resource. How else can we account for the fact that Switzerland, a country with few natural resources of any kind, has the highest per-capita income and living standard in the world? Imaginative and hopeful people exert their wills for their own benefit, and so, inevitably, for the benefit of us all.

Building Community

Just as blind obeisance can narcotize our creative powers, people who blindly follow the advice of experts can separate themselves from one another. Blind belief in the experts encourages us to act like isolated islands: the focus is on *my* risk factors for heart disease, *my* cholesterol numbers, *my* weight, *my* needs, *my* desires.

Social realities in the United States amplify the trend of isolation. Many Americans live alone or in nontraditional households and are cut off from the traditional social structures that once defined and gave meaning to life. More and more of us are spending time in superficial interactions. Intimacy, once taken for granted, is now difficult to achieve. The shelves of bookstores bulge with how-to manuals on ways to get close to spouses, children, and friends.

Many of our seemingly insoluble social problems are a direct result of the loss of a sense of community and responsibility. On my first trip to Japan, for example, I saw firsthand how a sense of community was being used to help prevent problems related to alcohol abuse. A Japanese judge sentenced two friends to prison for two years because they had "caused death by abandoning a person in a state of temporary illness due to advanced intoxication."

The two men had gone out drinking with a third friend. In their drunken state, the three had crossed some railroad tracks, and one of the men fell and lay on the tracks while the other two went on their way. An oncoming train killed the third man. The Japanese court ruled that when a person succumbs to the influence of alcohol, it is the responsibility of his friends to care for him until he regains self-control. I tried to adapt this concept of social responsibility to our individualistic American ethos in my alcohol abuse prevention efforts in the United States.

As a member of the Presidential Commission on Drunk Driving, I championed the concept of seller and server liability: making those who sell or serve alcohol beverages assume responsibility for the safety of drunk patrons. I created a training program to help servers and sellers interrupt abusive patterns of behavior. The program has been used in all fifty states and has trained hundreds of thousands of sellers, servers, and social hosts. The program, called Training for Intervention Procedures (TIPS), has been expanded to include the university community, the workplace, parents, and the elderly.

At first, an attractive incentive for people to participate in this program was the reduction in liability insurance premiums offered to establishments with trained personnel. Important as these discounts have been, the primary reason for the program's popularity is the sellers' and servers' own sense of enhanced professionalism and responsibility to their customers and their communities.

It was feared that patrons would become irate when a seller or server intervened in their private behavior. But trained servers have said that customers rarely react belligerently. Even individualistic Americans accept social limits on behavior. When customers are treated respectfully and not humiliated, they do not challenge the right of servers and sellers to set the rules in their own establishments. In fact, many customers appreciate the server's concern.

We can apply the principles such as the concern for others that underlie this alcohol abuse prevention program to any number of social problems. Social responsibility acknowledges that none of us acts in isolation. Our individual choices have social consequences.

Balancing our prickly American individualism and our deep need for one another is a challenge. The Jewish philosopher Hillel observed, "If I am not for myself, who will be for me? But if I am for myself alone, what am I?"

And What of the Naked Emperor?

A vital community draws on the talents of all its members. Even the experts have a positive role to play. Usually they are highly trained in specialized subjects, and within the bounds of those technical areas, their knowledge and skills are valuable. Only a dentist can fill a tooth. Only a lawyer can plead a case. Only a surgeon can remove a diseased gallbladder. We can choose to take what the experts can give us of value and discard their intrusive prescriptions.

One way to keep the experts in perspective is to remember that they are human—sometimes all too human. I recall that on my first day at Massachusetts General Hospital Benjamin Spock, the world-famous author on rearing children, gave a lecture to a roomful of his colleagues. I don't remember one word he said. All I can recall is that the great man gave his entire speech with his fly open.

Recalling a more personal memory of my friend Norbert Wiener really helps me keep my perspective. Preparing to meet him for the first time in Mexico in the 1950s, I was beside myself with ecstasy at the thought of meeting a true genius. I arranged to take him to lunch at an elegant, expensive restaurant far beyond my means. My excitement was so great that I reserved another table at the same restaurant so my wife and a friend could watch me figuratively sit at the feet of the great man.

But that is not what happened. At the time, Wiener was working on the first volume of his autobiography and was struggling to describe his relations with his brilliant but difficult father. Once he learned that I was a psychiatrist, he spent most of our lunch time literally crying about his father. This famous man, genius, and expert in his field reached out to me, a virtual stranger, for comfort.

My friendship with Wiener taught me that even a genius does not have all of the answers. More important, it also taught me not to underrate the value of my own expertise. My friend was an extraordinary man: he wrote the alphabet at eighteen months, entered Tufts College at nine, had his Ph.D. at seventeen, and began his career studying in London with the renowned philosopher and mathematician Bertrand Russell. Yet he often lamented that his father Leo, a genius in his own right, always claimed that any success Norbert enjoyed was the result of his rigorous training.

As a psychiatrist, I chose to dismiss this view as the fantasy of a genius child toward a genius father. But a few years after Norbert's death, I found a letter from Leo Wiener in Bertrand Russell's autobiography recommending Norbert to Russell. The letter explicitly stated that Leo considered Norbert to be an ordinary child who did well only because he had been well trained by his father. So much for my expert psychiatric opinion.

When we deal with experts, we must be like the child who sees the emperor for what he is—a pretentious man whose self-delusions drove him to parade in the buff; or see a brilliant humanist, who shaped the childrearing practices of a generation, lecture with his fly open; or see one of the important thinkers of the century weeping to a stranger in a restaurant.

Life without Self-Delusion

We want what people have always wanted, protection from our own fallibility, our own weakness, our own mortality. This desire helps to perpetuate our species. Recently I was awed by the raw honesty of my young grand-daughter Maria, who glibly summed up the human condition when she stated her life's aspirations: "I want to be a queen; I don't want to die; I want people to do what I tell them to."

Fortunately or unfortunately, I can't grant Maria her wishes, nor can the experts. Whatever advice, warnings, or formulas we follow, no one can make us exceptional, immortal, or omnipotent. By accepting the tenet that the experts cannot give us what we want, I hope we'll be able to give one another the courage to live without self-delusion.

Perhaps the greatest delusion of all is the notion that, individually and collectively, the human race is teetering on the brink of disaster. My common sense tells me that despite the barrage of news each day about the risks of daily life, and despite our many serious social, political, ecological, and economic problems, the earth and the human race are not on the verge of extinction. For every story that says we are running out of time by irreparably damaging our planet, there's another story that tells of an extraordinary scientific discovery, a new drug to treat a formerly intractable condition, a remarkable new movement in painting or sculpture, a groundbreaking new book or symphony or invention.

Whatever goes wrong in the world, we will still retain our most important asset: the infinite creativity and ingenuity of the human mind. I believe these ancient gifts that make man rise above all other animals will steer us through the maze of confusion fostered by the twentieth century's

135

bewildering succession of changes. Our challenge will be to find new ways to tap our wellspring of common sense and instinct for self-preservation. Meeting the challenge requires a commitment to look to ourselves for our own answers, because the spoon-feeding experts lead to our diminishment.

Don't ask me how to proceed once you've made that commitment, because I haven't a clue. What I do know, however, is that it is the journey not the destination that's important. Our search will begin in earnest when we are willing to embark on the journey.

The One and Only Expert

Although there are no certainties, no road maps, no easy answers that an outsider can give us, we do have some choices. Our major choice—to one degree or another—is to think and decide for ourselves. Although I have criticized some experts by saying how they tyrannize and exploit us, I will now speak of the awesome merits of the one expert who can help us—oneself.

Think about it for a moment: there has never been and never will be another you. Only you could have been born at that moment in time to the parents who conceived you. Only you could have undergone the countless experiences that were uniquely felt, sensed, seen, dreamed, and interpreted by you. Experts may make generalizations about groups and populations, but they can't describe (or even know) the specifics of you. Only you can make the choices that are right for you.

Plenty of your choices may be wrong, but remember the old adage: To err is human. Sam Walton, an extremely successful entrepreneur, when asked about his success, was reported to answer the interviewer's questions as follows:

Question: Mr. Walton, what was the secret of your success?

Answer: Right decisions.

Question: Mr. Walton, how did you manage to make the right decisions?

Answer: Experience.

Question: Mr. Walton, how did you come to get your experience?

Answer: Wrong decisions.

Even if it were possible for the experts to erase our human frailties and give us the perfect, disappointment-free world they promise, we probably wouldn't thank them for it. In 1955, I saw a Rod Serling half-hour television show in black and white that has haunted me ever since. In the first scene, a young bank robber is trying to escape from the scene of his crime, gun blazing. After a loud explosion, the TV screen momentarily goes blank. Then the young man reappears, asleep in a richly appointed bedroom.

As he awakens, his companion, a voluptuous young woman, asks him what he'd like to do. "Go to the races," he replies. When he gets there, he has an incredible winning streak. Every horse he bets on wins. Every woman he looks at falls for him. If he puts his finger in the coin-return box of a pay phone, it holds a coin. As the afternoon wears on, he becomes more and more frustrated with each success. Finally, he turns to his companion and complains, "I'm not sure I like being in heaven."

"Whoever said you were in heaven?" she replies.

Afterword

As I ponder the heart and soul and essence of this book, I am reminded that we come into this world as exquisitely refined creatures with a heart that works twenty-four hours a day, a brain that is curious and evolving every moment of every day—asleep or awake, an amazing physical system that functions automatically, and a host of features that make us unique. Added to this almost flawless machine is another feature that fortunately saves us from perfection: human error.

Recalling the innate beauty and potential of the human being is my prime reason for criticizing those people who try to control your life; I favor the only person who can ever be in control of you—yourself. I have no prescription or advice or manuals to help you on your journey through life. I hardly know what's right for me. What I can do is share my perspective with you so that, perhaps, somehow, somewhere, you can accept your brief moment in the sun—and in doing so overthrow the tyranny of experts.

First, come to terms with the undeniable fact that you are the *only* expert on you. Second, no one has any answers for getting through life; there are no formulas or recipes to follow. Third, there is no certainty, and there are no absolutes. Fourth, life is brief and death is everlasting. And fifth, everyone needs to live a little, having someone to love, something to do, and something to hope for.

I have lived most of my life by this perspective, oftentimes not consciously, and have benefitted greatly from it. I don't mean to say that I've had an easy life or have done everything right, because I haven't. My journey through life is not easy or worry free. I don't think there's a person alive who looks into his or her past and doesn't find times of sorrow, disappointment, and regret.

Whatever components influence our lives—such as parents, grandparents, siblings, friends, spouses, children, teachers, religious leaders, and neighbors; skin color, height, weight, intelligence, gender, and appearance; or any other real and imagined multiples that impinge on you—no one can change the past. We are what we are at any point in time, and change is inexorable.

In this afterword, I offer the reader a glimpse of my life, not as a smug autobiographical sketch entitled "Look at Me," but as a reflection of one person's observations, mistakes and all.

My father was an ebullient, outgoing person who covered his weaknesses by his openness with other people. He gave me unconditional love: He made me believe that I could achieve anything I wanted. Unconditional love, however, included a strapping on my bare bottom when he felt I deserved it.

My mother was a different sort. Strong of character, opinionated of mind, uncomfortable in unfamiliar circumstances, and a practitioner of ceaseless worry. She did not believe anything was possible. A generally negative approach to life was her magical elixir to ward off harm and bad luck. In spite of my mother's constant state of anxiety, she was overtly loving and giving.

I was an only child with a sister and brother; my sister is ten years older and my brother seven years older than I am. My mother became pregnant almost immediately after my brother's birth. She once told me that my father's sexual needs superseded any thoughts of possible unwanted pregnancies, and she sought out and received an illegal abortion. The abhorrence shown by the extended family to her "immoral" act was such that my mother was convinced she could never conceive again. However, I was born a few years later in 1924 to two uneducated immigrants (my siblings and I are first generation Americans).

I was a nuisance to my siblings (and I suspect everyone else who had to experience my presence). My parents had had it with child rearing when I came along. I got away with smart talking and smart assing my way through my early life. I was a child who was pretty of face, cowardly of character, afraid of being hurt, and I was told I was extremely selfish; I subsequently believed that I was incapable of caring for anyone but myself.

I grew up in an environment where strength, daring, and athletics were admired qualities. Unfortunately, I had none of these qualities. I can still see the kids I grew up with choosing sides for teams and worrying that they might get me.

The emphasis on physical activities forced me to focus on mental activities. I read a great deal and studied hard (for just slightly above average marks). But from early on, I knew I would become a medical doctor. My reasons were less than noble: Taking care of others, I reasoned, would prove that I was not selfish; and furthermore, in my milieu, becoming a medical doctor was the epitome of success and eternal respect for a Jewish immigrant's child. Realistically

141

the likelihood of becoming a doctor was as remote as my landing on the moon.

I was a coward, unpopular, and afraid of being hurt and rejected. I handled these fears and a low self-esteem by becoming obnoxious enough to ward off the slights of my peers. I behaved in a way that perpetuated my unpopularity. Just as adjusting to circumstances that I couldn't change caused me to develop my brain, adjusting to another negative, World War II, gave me a shot at becoming a doctor.

I worked as a shoe salesman and stockboy after school when I was thirteen: I earned seven dollars for forty hours a week and it was put aside to pay for college because the Great Depression had devastated my father and my family's resources, and seven dollars was big money. Another negative turned into a lucky positive for me when I bought the ugliest green, reversible trench coat with my first earnings, and this foolish purchase made me realize possessions did not matter.

By the time I was admitted to Tufts University, World War II had begun. Draft boards were siphoning up all able-bodied men and college life was bizarre. I was told the war effort needed doctors and I brazenly applied to medical school after *one* semester of college. I didn't have a ghost of a chance of getting into medical school, except for my father who had the brass to ask a wealthy but distant cousin for help. Harry Posner manufactured boxes for Rinso soap and other products and had contributed large amounts of money to Tufts Medical School. Again, the circumstances were fortuitous. My father and I met with cousin Harry who put in a good word.

Once medical school started, though, the old fears intensified. I was afraid the faculty would find out soon enough that I could not do the work and that I would be found out and thrown out. When the class assembled for the first session and the dean said, "Look to your right; look to your left; one of the three of you will not graduate," I knew for sure he meant me.

I did not do well. With feelings of ineptitude, my fear of being found out, and the sexual strivings for an older woman (who made me feel that I was the greatest man in bed who had ever lived), I barely got by. I think it's possible that I survived by convincing some of my professors that under the debris that was me was some medical worth.

What really made all the difference in my life and schooling was the accidental meeting of the girl who was to become my wife. I never dreamed that a scared rabbit like me could attract a woman of her natural beauty, verve, and talents. More important, my feelings for her were so overwhelmingly powerful that I allowed myself to believe, for the first time, that maybe, just maybe, I wasn't a totally selfish person.

My wife and I had a problem: she was an Irish Catholic girl and I was a Jewish boy from an orthodox background. For a Jew to marry an Irish Catholic in 1946 was the equivalent of a mixed marriage in the South in the 1930s.

I could not be dissuaded; this woman was everything I was not: beautiful, talented, daring, courageous, and fearless. And she seemed to like me (I learned later that my brain attracted her, not the rest of me). I wooed her with images of service on behalf of humankind in distant lands. I was lucky to win her as my wife, and I say unabashedly that if I have done anything respectable and worthwhile, Marion made me do it.

I went into psychiatry for two reasons: First, I became disillusioned with the medical profession's decreasing sensitivity to people and its increasing interest in money, and I believed psychiatry would allow me to care about people. Second, psychiatric residencies were the best-paying residencies in medicine, since few medical school graduates gave the specialty of psychiatry much value.

As luck would have it, when the Korean conflict erupted, I was called back to the Public Health Service (then a military entity) and sent to Mexico to serve as the physician for Americans serving in the *AFTOSA* program. The United States had set up the *AFTOSA* program in Mexico to prevent the possibility of hoof and mouth disease of cattle from jumping across the Rio Grande and infecting American herds.

My assignment was an example of government waste. When I got there the program was essentially over, and they didn't need me. So I wandered over to the National Institute of Cardiology and easily received a nonpaying research fellowship.

The reader might rightfully wonder why a psychiatrist was interested in cardiology. During my internship, I had come across a book that had impacted upon me mightily— Norbert Wiener's *Cybernetics*. Wiener, a genius and brilliant mathematician at MIT, had worked with Arturo Rosen-blueth, now head of the department of neurophysiology at the Cardiology Institute, on cybernetic theory, which, in the opinion of people more knowledgeable than I, was the forerunner of our present communication and technology breakthroughs. I went to the Cardiology Institute looking for Norbert Wiener.

The Rockefeller Foundation had given these two scientific giants a grant to work together, splitting the time between Mexico and Cambridge, Massachusetts. My luck was holding. Wiener was in Mexico when I applied for the fellowship, and I got to meet him. This chance encounter changed my life. Before meeting Norbert my sights were set on becoming a psychiatrist and comfortably spending the rest of my life in psychiatric practice in some fashionable suburb of New York such as New Rochelle.

But Wiener, like my father, believed in me and convinced me that I was suited for academic medicine. He wanted me close to him in Boston, so he arranged for me to get a fellowship in psychiatry at Harvard and Massachusetts General Hospital under Stanley Cobb when my tour of duty in Mexico was over.

Stanley Cobb, like Norbert Wiener, was good to me. He was the personification of New England Yankee achievement. He was crippled by severe arthritis, a stutterer, an outcast from all the specialties he was trained in: psychiatry, neurology, and neuropathology; Cobb, for some reason, believed in me. He nominated me as Harvard's representative for a Markle Scholarship over any number of highly talented people.

When my training was ending I wanted to stay on at the hospital. But staff jobs were scarce for Jews in WASP heaven (and I sure wanted to make it, neurotically and self-destructively, in WASP heaven).

Only one job was available; the State of Massachusetts had given the hospital the funds to start the third alcohol clinic in the state. No self-respecting psychiatrist wanted the job, least of all me. I did not care much for alcoholics, believing they were self-indulgent bums, but I took the job, and in a life full of negatives becoming positives, it was a fateful decision.

It was a fateful decision because the field was wide open. Not many people were interested in alcoholism in 1954 except for some who were themselves afflicted. There was no appreciable competition or threat to me. I could do my own thing without stepping on anyone's toes. The other doctors in the hospital were not threatened; it wasn't a

145

highly respected field of endeavor in medicine. The hospital was delighted somebody was doing the "dirty" work.

The clinic and I began to grow in notice, because the medical profession was finally beginning to treat alcoholic people with respect and care. More important, I began to realize that alcoholism with all of its attendant problems was a reflection of every social and health problem our society faces: ignorance, bias, hopelessness, unrealistic expectations, judgment, and the unnecessary infliction of pain.

Alcoholism became the fulcrum of the missionary zeal that I had courted my wife with a dozen or so years ago. I have no doubt now that I could never have sustained the personal discomfort that missionary medicine required. It was a fairy tale I told myself to make up for my underlying image of pathological selfishness. What greater way to rid oneself of selfish drives than by performing unselfish public deeds.

I went on to have three sons and a very satisfying career. I have six grandchildren, I have traveled widely, skied extensively, played tennis intensely, and written and lectured a lot. I started a federal agency. I have mingled with the rich and powerful, celebrities and achievers. And for better or worse, I myself am an expert.

My life and my experience have taught me several things. I like who and what I am, warts and all; I am comfortable with the phrase "I don't know"; and I am still discovering what is right for me; but only you, and you alone, can find what is right for you.

Notes and Sources

Preface

According to the FBI, 95 percent of the nearly 350,000 children reported missing nationwide each year are runaways. Almost all of the rest are taken by their noncustodial parent. Throughout the United States, fewer than one hundred children each year are kidnapped by strangers.

Daniel Defoe, "The Kentish Petition," addenda, l. 11. J. R. Moore, *A Checklist of the Writings of Daniel Defoe*, 1971.

Chapter 1

Bruce Ames, "Strong views on origins of cancer," *New York Times*, 5 July 1994, C9–10.

The ad on mammography was described in the article "Promoting Health Anxiety: Alarmist Advertising Exploits Popular Fears of Disease and Death" by Alison Bass in the health section of *Washington Post*, 15 January 1991.

Michael Schrage, "Welcome to the Year of Conspicuous Consumption of 'Health'," *Washington Post*, 4 January 1991.

Healthy People 2000, 1994 review, National Health Promotion and Disease Prevention Objectives, U.S. Department of Health and Human Services.

Daniel Goleman, "Use of drugs and lower cholesterol is tied to a higher depression risk," *New York Times*, 1 March 1995. Speaks of studies that found a correlation between lower cholesterol levels and increased death rate from suicide and other violent causes.

Gina Kolata, "Vitamin supplements are seen as no guard against diseases," *New York Times*, 14 April 1995, A1, A19. The study was supported by the National Cancer Institute and National Public Health Institute in Finland.

Kathryn E. Kelly, "Cleaning up EPA's dioxin mess," *Wall Street Journal*, 29 April 1995. Report on advisor panel of scientists who told the EPA that it had overstated the risks and it could not endorse their position.

"Double Vision: Twin Lab Finds Itself a Lucrative Niche in Health-Food Pills" by Yumiko Ono, *Wall Street Journal*, 8 August 1995. The article discusses the Blechman family's ability to sniff out health trends, make products quickly, and sell them with the benefits of little regulation.

Letter to the editor by J. R. Kaplan and Stephen B. Manucka was published in the September 1990 issue of the *British Medical Journal*.

Ames's recantation is discussed in "Heresy in the Cancer Lab," *Business Week*, 15 October 1990.

The dioxin test was conducted at the National Institute for Occupational Safety and Health and was published in the 24 January 1991 issue of the *New England Journal of Medicine*. M. A. Fingerhut, et al., "Cancer Mortality in Workers Exposed to 3-7-8-8-tetrachlorodibenzo-p-dioxin."

The Yale study is discussed in "Mortality Study Lends Weight to Patient's Opinion" by Daniel Goleman in the *New York Times* health section, 21 March 1991.

Ron Cowen of *Science News* described these and other examples of widespread use of medicinal herbs by a variety of animals in "Creature, Heal Thyself," *Washington Post*, 17 February 1991.

Information from Jean McCann's article "Can Physicians Watch Millions at HBP Risk?" *Medical Tribune*, 15 September 1982, 25.

Marcia Angell, "Assessing Health Information: Not All News Must Be Heeded," *Washington Post*, 4 December 1990.

Chapter 2

Back cover of *Children of Alcoholism: A Survivor's Manual* by Judith S. Seixas and Geraldine Youcha (New York: Harper and Row, 1985).

Stanton Peele, Ph.D., in a comprehensive and enlightening book called *Diseasing of America: Addiction Treatment Out of Control* (Lexington, Mass.: Lexington Books, 1989) devotes all of chapter 5 to discussing the reliability of various statistics on behavioral disorders. I am indebted to his work throughout this chapter.

Tom Lutz, *American Nervousness, 1903* (Ithaca, N.Y.: Cornell University Press, 1993).

Charles L. Whitfield, M.D., *Healing the Child Within* (Deerfield Beach, Fla.: Health Communications, Inc., 1987).

For further examples of the inadequacy of treatment versus time and self-care, see Stanton Peele, *Diseasing of America*, chapter 7.

This study on adolescent suicide conducted by David Shaffer of Columbia University College of Physicians and Surgeons was published in the 26 December 1990 issue of *Journal of the American Medical Association*, "Adolescents suicide attempters. Response to sucide prevention programs."

Janet Frame's life was brought to the screen in 1991 by New Zealand director Jane Campion in the film *An Angel at My Table*.

Robert Lindner, *Must You Conform?* (New York: Grove Press, 1956) 173.

Gail Sheehy, *Passages: Predictable Crises of Adult Life* (New York: Bantam Books, 1974).

A similar point is made by the popular counselor and theologian John Bradshaw in *Healing the Shame that Binds You* (Deerfield Beach, Fla.: Health Communications, Inc., 1988).

Chapter 3

Cynthia Crossen, *Tainted Truth*: *The Manipulation of Fact in America* (New York: Simon & Schuster, 1994).

Cited in Stanton Peele, *Diseasing of America*: Addiction Treatment Out of Control (Lexington, Mass.: Lexington Books, 1989), chapter 2.

Chapter 4

Robyn E. Blumner, "Prosecuting the Persecuted Addicted Mothers-to-Be," *Miami Herald*, 28 April 1991.

An extensive discussion of testing women for prenatal drug use is included in "Using Pregnancy to Control Women" by Ruth Hubbard, a retired professor of biology at Harvard University, published in the October 1990 issue of *Sojourner*.

Two attorneys, one living in Germany and one living in the United States, detailed the contrasting policies of the German and American governments in a letter to the editor published in the *Washington Post*, 13 November 1990.

A discussion of "Halloween sadists" and other obsessive attitudes toward protecting children appears in Stanton Peele, *Diseasing of America*: *Addiction Treatment Out of Control* (Lexington, Mass.: Lexington Books, 1989), chapter 9.

This study of dyslexia by researchers at the Yale University School of Medicine was published in the 16 January 1992 issue of *New England Journal of Medicine*.

Chapter 5

Joel Achenbach, "Biosphere 2: Bogus New World?" *Washington Post*, 8 January 1992.

Barbara Holland, *Endangered Pleasures* (Boston: Little, Brown, 1995). The author likes smoking: thinks cigarettes are sexy and companionable.

Without them, she contends, men in a group become disconnected, "left standing there like an arrangement of stones." She does not doubt they are bad for your health, but they make society work better.

Joyce Price, "Second-hand smoke's dangers doubts," *Washington Times*, 27 November 1995. The Congressional Research Service reports had OSHA combined results of all studies that have investigated the issue "it seems likely that it would have found no increased lung-cancer risk from occupational EST exposure."

The medical literature on 60-Hertz was analyzed by *New Yorker* staff writer Paul Brodeur in his 1989 book entitled, *Currents of Death: Power Lines, Computer Terminals, and the Attempt to Cover Up Their Threat to Your Health* (New York: Simon and Schuster).

These risk estimates are taken from the comprehensive study by Richard Doll and Richard Peto, "The Causes of Cancer: Quantitative Estimates of Avoidable Risks of Cancer in the United States Today," *Journal of the National Cancer Institute*, 66, no. 6 (June 1981).

The debate on global warming has not entirely escaped the attention of the press. See, for example, the *Washington Post* articles by William Booth: "Global Warming Continues, but Cause is Uncertain" and "Conference on Global Warming to Seek Agreement on Response."

Reporter Howard Kurtz discusses the controversy over the National Acid Precipitation Assessment Program report in "Is Acid Rain a Tempest in News Media Teapot?" *Washington Post*, 14 January 1991.

Susan Seligson, columnist for *In Health* magazine, cited these statistics with amusement in her December/January 1992 column, referring to the dangers of high fashion as "*de rigueur* mortis."

This point about the unforeseen benefits of nuclear energy has also been made by Dixie Lee Ray, a scientist and former governor of Washington state.

Chapter 6

A version of this story is related in the *Little, Brown Book of Anecdotes*, Clifton Fadiman, general editor (Boston: Little, Brown, 1985).

These findings on the alcoholism gene were critiqued extensively by Stanton Peele in "The Second Thoughts about a Gene for Alcoholism," *Atlantic Monthly*, August 1990.

This critical look at genetic findings in alcoholism appeared in an editorial by Ernest Noble, et al., "Dopamine D-2 receptor gene and alcoholism" in the *Journal of the American Medical Association*, October 1991, 265, 267–68.

Thomas A. Pearson, M.D., Ph.D., and Paul Terry, M.P.H., "What to Advise Patients about Drinking Alcohol: The Clinician's Conundrum," *Journal of the American Medical Association*, 28 September 1994. Editorial stating that 80,294 additional coronary heart disease deaths would occur from a nationwide abstinence from alcohol.

Joe C. Christian, M.D., Ph.D., et al., "Self-Reported Alcohol Intake and Cognition in Aging Twins," *Journal of Studies on Alcohol*, 56 (1995): 414–16.

This comment was made by Gordis in his plenary lecture to the International Society for Biomedical Research on Alcoholism in Toronto, Canada, in June 1990.

In an interview with Shari Roan of the *Los Angeles Times*, psychiatrist Roland Summit of the Harbor-UCLA Medical Center in Torrance, Calif., blames the pressures for conformity on Tardieu, Ferenczi, and Freud. Excerpts from the interview appeared in "The Lingering Trauma of Childhood Sex Abuse," in the health section of *Washington Post*, 4 December 1990.

This quotation, drawn from the 1912 biography of this Italian noblewoman of the Reformation era, is cited in *The Quotable Woman, From Eve to 1799* (New York: Facts on File Editions, 1985).

Malcolm Gladwell, "How Driving Under the Influence of Society Affects Traffic Deaths," *Washington Post*, 2 September 1991.

Tom Kando, a professor of sociology and criminal justice at California State University in Sacramento, discussed the stresses experienced by California police officers in "LA. Debate—Police Are Also Victims,"

Wall Street Journal, 19 March 1991. Another *Wall Street Journal* article, published 11 November 1991 ("Hidden Casualties: Drug War's Emphasis on Law Enforcement Takes a Toll on Police" by Alex Kotlowitz), explores the extreme toll taken on police officers by the violence that accompanies the "war on drugs."

Amy Friedman, letter to the editor, "We choose the risks," *New York Times*, 5 August 1995.

Niccolò Machiavelli, *Discourses on the First Ten Books of Titus Livius*, chapter LIII (Florence, Italy, 1513).

Joel Achenbach, "The Age of Unreality: Milli Vanilli and the Phony-Baloney Factor," *Washington Post*, 20 November 1990.

In his intelligent and enlightening 1971 biography of Einstein, *Einstein: The Life and Times* (New York: Avon Books), Ronald W. Clark spends most of chapter 12 discussing Einstein's many statements on this same theme and elaborating on the great genius's profound unease over the acceptance of subatomic chaos by many of the physicists who followed him. Ironically, many physicists in the 1980s began to have the same discomfort that Einstein expressed. Many orthodox physicists now believe that fundamental laws *will* inevitably be found that will eliminate the appearance of randomness at the subatomic level.

Chapter 7

Robert, Lord Salisbury, letter to Lord Lytton, 15 June 1877, cited in *The Life of Robert, Marquis of Salisbury*, by Lady Gwendolyn Cecil.

Nicholas Murray Butler, commencement address, Columbia University (n.d.), 1931.

The American Museum of Natural History's enlightened response to the barosaurus controversy came to my attention in an article by Don Lessen in the *Boston Globe*, 10 December 1990.

Index

AA. See Alcoholics Anonymous
abduction, xii, 147
abnormality, 29–30
abstinence, 76, 152
abuse: alcohol, 131–32; drug, 76;
  fetal, 67–69; sexual, 115, 152
accidents, automobile, 56, 116, 152
accountability, 97–98
Achenbach, Joel, 81, 120, 150, 153
acid rain, 87–88, 151
activists, radical, 96–97
addiction, 93
adolescents. See teen drinking; teen
  pregnancy; teen suicide
advertising, 77; alcohol, 53–54;
  "Just Say No," 76; mammography, 1, 147; tobacco products,
  92–95; Woodsy the Owl, 83
advocacy: as institution, 91–92;
  natural life cycle of, 83–84
advocacy groups, 77
advocates: accountability of, 97–98;
  public health, 92–95
affirmative action, 78

Agent Orange, 15
AIDS, 76
Alar, 92
alcohol: advertising, 53–54, 77;
  blood concentrations, 55–56;
  control of consumption, 50–52;
  fetal alcohol effects, 66–67; irresistible force of, 49–50; seller
  and server liability, 132. See also
  drinking
alcohol abuse: prevention, 131–32;
  Training for Intervention Procedures (TIPS), 132
alcohol beverage industry, 53–54,
  96
alcohol and drug treatment industry, 35
alcohol experts, 47–61
Alcoholics Anonymous (AA),
  28–29, 31, 38, 130
alcoholism: children of, 23, 149;
  definition of, 37; gene, 110,
  152; treatment of, 94

155

156

About the Author

Morris E. Chafetz, M.D., is the founding director of the National Institute on Alcohol Abuse and Alcoholism (NIAAA) in the U.S. Department of Health and Human Services, where he served for five years. Prior to his government service, Dr. Chafetz served as associate clinical professor of psychiatry at Harvard Medical School, director of clinical psychiatric services, and chief of the alcohol clinic at Massachusetts General Hospital in Boston. In 1982, Dr. Chafetz was appointed by President Ronald Reagan to the Presidential Commission on Drunk Driving as chairman of its Education and Prevention Committee. Today he serves on the Board of Directors of the National Commission Against Drunk Driving.

Dr. Chafetz is president and founder of the Health Education Foundation, an organization that relates health to lifestyle.

In 1995 he was inducted into the Safety and Health Hall of Fame International for his numerous pioneering accomplishments, such as removing the stigma of alcoholism, and for developing programs to prevent alcohol abuse;

a fellow of the Royal Society of Health; a recipient of the Mt. Airy Gold Medal Award for Distinguished Service to Psychiatry; past Sigma Xi National Lecturer; and the holder of many national and international awards and honors.

Dr. Chafetz has written and collaborated on numerous articles and books, including *Drink Moderately and Live Longer: Understanding the Good of Alcohol* (Madison Books, 1995). He serves on numerous national and international boards dealing with health, psychiatry, and alcoholism, and appears on television, radio, and lecture platforms.